Access 7
Further Skills

A progressive course for users

Sue Coles

Department of Business and Management Studies
Crewe and Alsager Faculty
Manchester Metropolitan University

Jenny Rowley

School of Management and Social Sciences
Edge Hill University College

Letts
1997

Acknowledgements

This book would not have been completed without the support that the authors have received, during its production, from many of their colleagues and family. They are particularly grateful to husbands Martyn and Peter, children Helen, Lynsey, Shula and Zeta, who had to make do with even less of their time than usual.

The computer program Microsoft Access 7 is copyrighted by the Microsoft Corporation, all rights reserved. Screen displays from Microsoft Access 7 are reprinted with permission. Microsoft Access 7 is a registered trademark of the Microsoft Corporation.

A CIP record for this book is available from the British Library.

ISBN 1 85805 217 3

Editorial and production services: Genesys Editorial

Typeset by Goodfellow & Egan Ltd, Cambridge

Printed in Great Britain by Martins the Printers, Berwick upon Tweed

Contents

iv

About Access

Access is a powerful and exciting database management system for Windows 95. It provides standard data management features

About this book

Aims

This book is intended for students on a wide variety of business studies and other courses who need to learn about databases and their application through the use of Microsoft Access, one of the industry standard database packages. The book assumes no prior experience of other database packages.

Although this book is specifically designed for business studies students the approach will be equally applicable to students, on many courses in further and higher education, who need to learn about databases.

This book is designed for business studies students on a wide range of courses, including BTEC National, BTEC Higher and undergraduate courses in business studies, accountancy, computing and information systems.

Scope

This set of units has been specifically designed for students who will benefit from a straightforward introduction to databases in the context of a specific database package. The aim is not to be comprehensive, but rather selective.

The active-learning approach

In this book you will be introduced to the basics of databases and database design through a series of applications oriented tasks. These tasks are based on the operations of one organisation, Chelmer Leisure and Recreation Centre. A series of self contained but interrelated units takes you through the design of a database for Chelmer Leisure and Recreation Centre. Each unit comprises a series of tasks. As each new function is introduced, the book explains both why the function is useful and how to use it.

The approach does not assume any previous knowledge of databases or the Windows 95 environment. However, if you are familiar with the Windows 95 environment, and, in particular other Microsoft Office products such as Word, Excel and Powerpoint, you will find your road into Access to be much more intuitive than if you are not familiar with these related products. Equally, if you have some familiarity with other database products you may find the database concepts that are introduced in this book easier to grasp.

The approach is designed not only to introduce Access but also to offer a conceptual framework for the use and design of databases that will encourage the development of skills transferable to other applications.

The learning material requires little, if any, input by lecturers, and can therefore be used in programmes based on independent learning. You will learn by practising the commands and techniques.

The text is selective and does not deal with all the features in detail, but takes you step-by-step to a level at which you will be readily able to use the help Answer Wizard to master further features.

Getting started

Students who have not used a Windows program before should first read through Quick Reference 1 Basic Windows Operations which summarises the key features of the Windows environment, and then turn to An overview of Access. Students who are familiar with the Windows environment can move straight to An overview of Access.

Each unit commences with a summary of the objectives to be achieved and the skills to be gained. Each unit is divided into a number of activities. Within each activity, instructions on how to perform operations, and tasks which ask you to perform the operations. Series of related units conclude with integrative tasks which offer you the opportunity to practice your newly acquired skills further. These tasks have minimal instructions.

This book may be used as a basis for independent study or for class activities. In either instance it is important to:

■ work methodically through the tasks in the order in which they are presented. Data entered in earlier exercises may be re-used in later tasks.

■ take time for rest and reflection and break learning into manageable sessions

■ think about what you are doing

■ expect to make mistakes; think about the consequences of any mistakes and learn from them

■ use the integrative tasks at the end of unit series as a means of testing whether you have understood the earlier concepts and tasks.

Conventions

The following conventions have been adopted to distinguish between the various objects on the screen:

Buttons are shown as: **Save**

Menu items and Dialog box names are shown as: **Print**

Keys on the keyboard are shown as *Ctrl /A*

Filenames are shown as: **CHELMER LEISURE**

Names of fields, tables and other items created by the user are shown as **Members**

Text to be typed in is shown as: *Membership*

(Note that text can be typed in upper or lower case.)

(d.) indicates text that gives a definition of a term. Note that all definitions are also included in the Glossary.

indicates a tip providing a helpful hint or short-cut method.

indicates a cautionary note.

indicates a cross reference.

Lecturers' disk

A 3½" disk is available (free of charge to lecturers recommending the book as a course text) containing files of data for completing the tasks, plus the reports and queries produced via the tasks in the text. It can be used as a shortcut to avoid lengthy keying in of data and as a means of checking the outcomes of the tasks. The disk, or selected files from it, can be made available to students to allow them to check their own work.

Please apply to the publishers on college headed paper or telephone 0181 740 2266 for further details.

An overview of Access

All students, except those who have some experience of Access, should read this module. *Quick Reference 1*, towards the end of this book, reviews the basic features of Windows for the benefit of inexperienced users or as a ready reference for those who may have forgotten some of the basic features. It also introduces mouse techniques and acts as a summary of the terminology used throughout these units.

A tour of the Access window and the database window

It is worth studying the two basic windows in Access, the Access window and the Database window, for a few moments before trying to make use of Access. This section can be used as a ready reference and returned to later as necessary.

The Access window

When you first start Access, the Access window shown in FIGURE 1.1 is displayed. This window is used to open a database or to perform other tasks that are not possible once a database is open. The window has the following components:

Component	Description
Title bar	Shows that you are in Microsoft Access
Access control menu (in the very top left hand corner)	If you click on this box a menu with commands for sizing and moving the Access window, switching to other applications and closing Access is displayed
Access main menu	Shows the two pull-down menus **File** and **Help**
Toolbar	Shows the help icon, which can be used to call help quickly
Status bar (at the bottom of the screen)	Shows the status of the system, and whether switches such as NUM for Number Lock are on or off

FIGURE 1.1

The Database window

Once you have opened a database, a window like the one in FIGURE 1.2 is displayed. This window allows you to access any object (table, query, form, report, etc) in the database by clicking on one of the object 'tabs'. Initially the Table tab is selected and a window displays all tables in the database.

FIGURE 1.2

When the Database window is open, the Access window has the following components:

- Title bar

- Access control menu

- Database window main menu, which shows a few more pull-down menus than the Access window, specifically, **File**, **Edit**, **View**, **Insert**, **Tools**, **Window** and **Help**.

- Toolbar, which shows the icons for the creation of new objects. The icons vary depending on the object that you are working on. For example, when working on a table there are toolbar options for choosing a datasheet or a design view. When designing a macro, there are icons for single-step mode, displaying conditions and macro names. All toolbar choices have equivalent menu selections.

- Status bar. Messages are displayed on the left of the status bar; for example, Ready. Modes are displayed on the right; for example, OVR indicates that overtype mode has been selected.

Help

Both help and tutorials are available for Access. There are four main methods of getting into the help system:

1 Pull down the **Help** menu and select either **Microsoft Access Help Topics** or **Answer Wizard**. If you choose the Answer Wizard then type in your question and click on **Search** .

2 At any time you can press *F1* to get help on whatever you are doing at that moment.

3 In most dialog boxes there is a help button on the title bar. Click on this button (it has a question mark on it) and then click on the area of the dialog box for which you want an explanation.

4 Press *Shift+F1*. The cursor changes to a pointer with a question mark after it and it can be used to point to anything. Clicking on that object will then bring up help. For instance, in this way you may get help on the meaning of all of the items in the status bar. To remove the question mark press *Shift+F1* again.

What is an Access database?

Access is a database management system, which provides a means of storing and managing data or information. Microsoft refers to Access as a relational database product since it allows you to relate data from several different sets or tables. The purist would recognise that Access does not meet all of the criteria of a true relational database, but it is a sufficiently close approximation to be considered as a relational database product for the purposes of this book.

An Access database comprises all of the tables of data and all associated objects, such as screen forms and report forms, macros, program modules and queries.

Note: the use of the term database in connection with Access is broader than that encountered in earlier database products such as dBase IV, where only the data itself 3 is considered to be part of the database. For example, you may have an employee database, a client database and a supplier database. Each database is a separate file, and there will also be additional files for reports and screen forms.

Tables

Access stores data in tables that are organised by rows and columns. The basic requirement for a database is that you have at least one table.

Columns represent fields of information, or one particular piece of information that can be stored for each entity in the table.

Rows contain records. A record contains one of each field in the database.

Generally each major set of information in a database is represented by a table. There might, for instance, be a supplier table, a client table and an employee table.

We will return later to the issue of how data might be organised in tables, and how relationships can be defined between tables so that tables can be used together, in such a way, for instance, that data from more than one table can be shown in a report.

Queries

Queries are used to select records from a database. Access has three different types: select, action and parameter.

Select queries are the standard type of query. They are questions that you may wish to ask about entries in fields. They choose records from a table and store them in a table called a dynaset. Queries are specified by completing entries in the Query-by-Example (QBE) window. It is possible to specify complex combinations of criteria in order to select a specific set of records.

Action queries update values in a database table. They can be used to change an entire group of records, as in, for example, the removal of all records for former employees.

Parameter queries allow you to change the criteria for a query each time you use it. Access prompts for criteria entries with the QBE grid. They are a useful way of creating an environment for end users where users complete dialog boxes instead of a QBE grid.

Reports

Reports are used to print information from a number of records. Reports can show the data from either a table or a query. In addition to records, they may show summary information relating to the records displayed. Graphs created using Microsoft Graph may be added to reports.

Screen forms

Screen forms can be used to customise the way in which records from tables or queries are presented on screen. They help to provide a user-friendly interface for the addition of new records or the editing of existing ones. Subforms allow you to display related records from another table at the same time.

Controls are placed on a form to display fields or text. Text on the form acts as labels to controls and headings. The appearance of text on a form can be changed by changing the font or adding bold or italic emphasis. Text can also be shown as raised or sunken, or displayed in a specific colour, and lines and rectangles can be added to give the form a pleasing appearance. Controls, attached labels, form sections and the form itself all have properties that can be changed.

Macros

Macros are a series of steps or keystrokes that you record; you use macros by pressing just one or two keys. Examples of potential uses of macros are:

■ to add a button to a form so that it will open a second form

■ to create custom menus and pop-up forms for data collection.

Modules

Modules are programs or sets of instructions designed to perform a specific task or series of tasks. Modules are written in Access Basic code, the programming language provided with Access.

Task 1: Questions

Answer the following questions:

1 What is the difference between a report and a screen form?

2 What types of queries may be used in Access?

3 What is a table? What is the relationship between a table and a database?

4 Give an example of when you might use a macro.

Defining a new database, creating tables

What you will learn in this unit

This unit focuses on the creation of an Access database file. This file is used to store all of the components of an Access database, which you will be creating as you work through these units. At the end of this unit you should:

■ appreciate the reasons for analysing data before creating a database

■ be able to define a new database

■ be able to retrieve this database

■ understand that, within a database, data is kept in tables and that there is usually more than one table in a database

■ understand that the tables in a database can be related or linked together.

Before a database can be created careful thought needs to be given to deciding upon the data that should be held and planning the way in which it is to be organised. This is known as data analysis, and you will be introduced to its basic concepts in this unit.

Data analysis

A database is used for storing data that can be used by a system. A system is not easily defined, although systems abound in society and nature. Your body has many systems, of which the nervous system and digestive system are examples. In society there are legal systems, political systems, educational systems, tax systems, etc. Organisations may have order systems, management information systems, product information systems, personnel data systems, sales marketing systems, etc. Libraries have cataloguing systems and information retrieval systems. In general terms, systems can be viewed as being concerned with taking inputs or resources, executing some form of regulated change, and achieving results or outputs. Systems often need access to data to act upon their inputs; if this data information is easily accessible, for example via a well-designed database, then the system will perform well.

Data or systems analysts are highly trained individuals who design information systems, of which databases usually form a major part. They use their skills to determine how to organise the data in the tables in the system's databases. It is not the intention of this book to impart analysis skills, but to give you a practical insight into the building of a database.

We shall be considering the database needs of a small leisure centre. Data is recorded about various things, such as membership details, court and course bookings, financial information, etc. The information about these different things, or entities, may be kept in tables in the database. If data from more than one table are required to be retrieved then the tables can be linked or related together, as will be explained in a later unit.

A table generally holds data about one 'thing' or entity. There are usually several or many instances of this particular 'thing', for example, the members of the leisure centre. A members' table would hold details about each member.

Records and fields

For each member there is a separate record in the table. Each record is composed of data about the member, such as name, address and so on. Each piece of data within the record is known as a field. In the opening units we will see how each field in a record needs to be defined before data can be entered into the record. Fields are given names to describe the kind of data they will eventually hold. It is important to distinguish between the name of a field and the data contained by that field. For example, the field named **Lastname** will hold people's surnames, such as Harris. The field names can be considered to be the column headings in the table, and each row in the table is a separate record. Therefore, each record in the table will have fields with the same name but containing different data. We shall also see that the size and the type of data that fields will contain need to be defined so that Access can store the data in the table correctly.

Defining a new database

A new database is used to store all of the tables, queries, forms and reports that belong to the system. To begin with, a database will hold the tables of data needed for the system. An Access file differs from traditional PC databases in that it can contain all of the tables, forms, reports, queries, macros etc that belong to a database. The one you are about to create awaits the inclusion of these as you learn to create them.

Task 1: Defining the Chelmer Leisure database

1   Choose File-New Database.

2   Double-click on the Blank Database icon.

3   In the File-New Database dialogue box, in the Save in box select the drive and directory in which you wish to store your database.

   If you do not change directory then your database is likely to be stored in the Access directory or in the **MY DOCUMENTS** folder in Windows 95.

3   In the File name box give the database the filename **CHELMER LEISURE**.

   Access will give it the extension of .mdb.

4   Click the Create button.

Access, as it is running in the Windows 95 environment, allows you to use long descriptive filenames. The complete path to the file, including drive letter, folder path name and filename, can contain up to 255 characters. Any characters may be used except the following: * ? ; \ / : " | < >. You cannot use a period (full stop) except to separate the filename from the extension. Note that Access stores all tables, forms, queries, reports etc in this one file.

Closing and opening a database

When you have finished working with the database you can close it using **File-Close**. If you have made changes that you have not saved then Access will prompt you to save them.

To open an existing database use **File-Open Database** or click on the Open Database icon on the toolbar. Select the drive and directory in which your database is stored, if necessary, select the filename and click on the **Open** button.

When you have finished working with Access you can close the application using **File-Exit**. Next time you start Access you will see your database listed in the **'Open an Existing Database'** section of the **Microsoft Access** dialogue box. Simply double-click on it to open the database.

Task 2: Closing and opening the Chelmer Leisure database

1   To close the database choose
    File-Close.

2   To open the database choose   In the **Open** dialog box select the drive
    File-Open Database.   and directory in which your database is
                                               stored.

3   Select the file **CHELMER LEISURE**
    from the list below the Look in box.

4   Click on the **Open** button.

5   To close Access choose **File-Exit**.

6   To open Access and choose an
    existing database, start Access by
    clicking on its icon.

7   Select the file **CHELMER LEISURE**
    from the list in the 'Open an
    Existing Database' section.

Understanding relationships between tables

Having created the database, the next step is to create the tables that go into it. How do you decide what constitutes a table and the sort of data it should contain? First consider the nature of the Chelmer Leisure and Recreation Centre.

A leisure centre basically needs a building, staff and people who use it. Often the facilities are cheaper for members of a leisure centre, and some centres require that you become a member before you can use the facilities. When a person joins the centre details about that person are obtained. Details about the staff who work at the centre will be needed so that they can be paid correctly. Details about the bookings of various rooms, halls and courts in the centre will be required so that the building is used efficiently. If the centre has a bar or cafe then details about food and drink kept in stock would need to be kept as well as, for example, sales records.

Let's look at the membership data in more detail. What sort of information will the centre be asking for on the membership form? Apart from name and address, date of birth is useful for targeting advertising to specific groups, e.g. senior citizens. Also, knowing something about the sporting interests of the member is useful. The information that Chelmer Leisure and Recreation Centre requires about each new member is shown in the following table:

Lastname

Firstname

Title

Street

Town

County

Post Code

Telephone No

Occupation

Date of Birth

Date of Joining

Date of Last Renewal

Sporting Interests

Smoker

Sex

The names in the table are the names of each piece or field of information. Before issuing a membership card, the centre will allocate a membership number, which is different from any other member's number, and will charge a membership fee. The centre offers different categories of membership, for which different fees are charged. Therefore, it is necessary to have two additional fields: **membership number** and **membership category**.

The centre will need to hold data about the current fees charged for each category of membership. This forms another table in our system, the membership category table:

Category No

Category Type

Membership Fee

To discover the fee that a member has paid by matching his or her membership category with the category number in the membership category table, the information in the two tables can be linked. This is known as relating the tables; by creating links between them they appear to be one table.

One advantage of using more than one table is that less storage space is required. Consider the situation where there is no membership category table and the information about category type and membership fee is stored in the table containing the members' information. Say there are 500 members: 500 membership category descriptions and 500 membership fee details will need to be stored. If, on the other hand, there are two tables, then there will be 500 category identification numbers, which need only be one digit long, and, assuming that there are six categories, six category identification numbers, six descriptions and six fee details. Another advantage is that the fees can be amended and the new data is available throughout the database simultaneously, so that when a new member joins or membership is renewed the correct fee details are used.

Two other tables forming part of the Chelmer Leisure and Recreation Centre system that we will be building are concerned with bookings of the rooms, halls and courts, and with the classes that are held. The centre will need to keep track of bookings of rooms to prevent double booking and to schedule classes. Rooms can be booked either by members or by a class, so there is a link between a member and a room booking and a link between a class and a room booking. The **Bookings** table and the **Classes** table are shown below:

Booking No	Class No
Room/Hall/Court	Class Day
Member/Class	Class Time
Member No	Class Tutor
Class No	Class Activity
Date	Male/Female/Mixed
Time	

FIGURE 2.1 shows the relational database used by our system for Chelmer Leisure and Recreation Centre. It shows how the four tables – the **Membership** table, the **Categories of Membership** table, the **Classes** table and the **Bookings** table – are linked. Each table is composed of records, and the fields in each table are listed in the boxes.

The fields in bold italics are known as primary key fields. You will be introduced to these in Unit 3.

Note: this is just one possible database structure that could be used for part of the system at Chelmer Leisure and Recreation Centre. The total system would be more complex, and a number of alternative database structures are also possible. The best database structure for a given application depends upon the way in which the database is to be used.

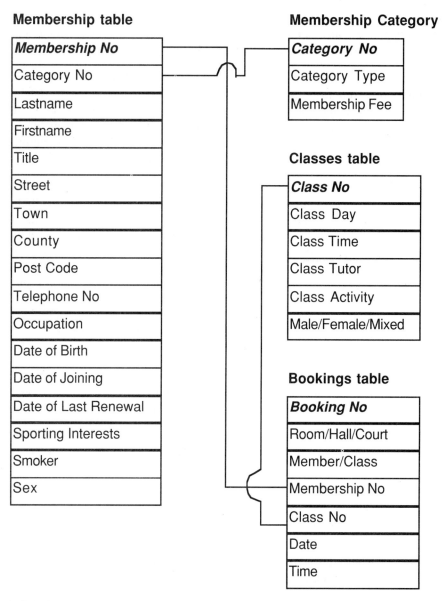

FIGURE 2.1

Task 3: Creating and linking tables

The centre will need to have details of the class tutors that it employs. Design a tutors' table on paper by considering the fields that will comprise the records in this table. How could this table be linked in with the tables in FIGURE 2.1?

Choosing data types

The first stage in building the database is to define the tables; that is, to name them and to define the names of the fields that will be contained in each table's records. The next stage is to define the type of data to be stored in each of the fields. No data has yet been entered but, before it can be, Access needs to know what sort of data to expect. Take the member's surname: first, you need to tell Access the field name, i.e. Lastname, and you also need to tell Access whether the data is text, numeric, date/time etc before you can actually start entering people's names!

Every field in your table will be of a particular data type. For example, a name is alphanumeric text, a price would be currency and a date would have a date data type. The data type that you choose for your field determines the kind and range of values that can be entered into it and the amount of storage space available in the field. Select the appropriate data type for each field. For example, you will probably define most fields in a table of names and addresses as text fields.

There are likely to be instances where a text field should be used when the data is numbers. Fields such as telephone numbers or employee works numbers that contain only digits should be defined as text fields. The reason for this is that there is no need to do calculations with telephone numbers or employee works numbers. Often telephone area codes start with a zero, which is not allowed in a true number. Employee works numbers may also start with one or more zeros (known as leading zeros). So, reserve the number data type for fields on which you want to perform calculations.

The table below lists the data types available in Access and their uses.

Data type	Use for ...
Text	Text and numbers. A text field can contain up to 255 characters. Examples: names and addresses, class activity.
Memo	Lengthy text and numbers. A memo field can contain up to 32,000 characters. Example: comments about a hotel in a travel company's database.
Number	Numerical data on which you intend to perform mathematical calculations, except calculations involving money. Set the FieldSize property to define the specific number data type. Example: number of items in stock.
Date/Time	Dates and times. A variety of display formats are available, or you can create your own. Example: date of joining.
Currency	Money. Don't use the number data type for currency values because numbers to the right of the decimal may be rounded during calculations. The currency data type maintains a fixed number of digits to the right of the decimal. Example: membership fee.

Data type	Use for ...
Counter	Sequential numbers automatically inserted by Microsoft Access. Numbering begins with one. Makes a good primary key field. The counter data type is compatible with the number data type with the FieldSize property set to Long Integer. Example: membership number.
Yes/No	Yes/No, True/False, On/Off. Example: smoker/non-smoker.

Task 4: Choosing data types

Think about the following questions:

1   What would be the effect of rounding on currency (money) data?

2   What data type do you think you would choose for the following fields?
>   Category No
>   Lastname
>   Street
>   Telephone No
>   Date of Birth
>   Sporting Interests

3   Later we suggest that you use a Yes/No field for Sex. Explain this!

4   Why would you use a text field for a post code?

Defining a new table

What you will learn in this unit

This unit focuses on the creation of a database table. The creation of a table requires the definition of the fields in the table. Each field requires a name to distinguish it from the other fields, and the type of data to be stored in the field also needs to be defined. At the end of this unit you should:

■ know the component parts of a table

■ be able to create a table

■ be able to define data types for fields.

Defining a new table

This activity takes the form of a task in which the membership table will be defined. In the task the fields will be set up so that they correspond to the type of data that will be stored in those fields.

Task 1: Creating a new table

1   The database window should
    be active.

This is indicated by a blue title bar if you are using the standard Windows colours.

2   The **Tables** 'tab' should be selected,
    as shown in the illustration. If it is not,
    then click on it.

3 Click on the **New** button in the table window to display the **New Table** dialogue box.

4 Select **Design View** from the list and click on the **OK** button to display the **Table Design** window.

The **Table Design** window allows you to define the structure of your table. By filling in the **Field Name, Data Type** and **Description** cells and by setting **Field Properties** the structure of the table is defined. This is described in Task 2.

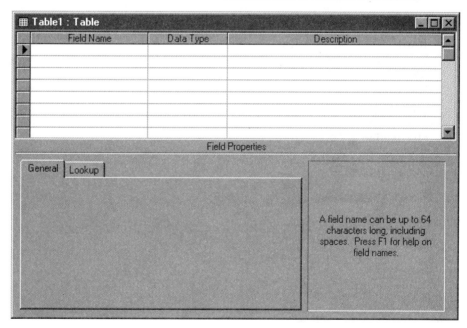

Task 2: Defining the fields in a table

In this task the fields for the **Membership** table will be defined and the name, data type and description will be entered into the table design window. You should be able to complete this task by following the instructions, but additional notes are also given in the activities described in the following few pages, which you may wish to consult. The membership table is defined as follows:

Field Name	Data Type	Description
Membership No	AutoNumber	Automatic membership numbering
Category No	Number	Categories are 1, Senior; 2, Senior Club; 3, Junior; 4, Junior Club; 5, Concessionary; 6, Youth Club
Lastname	Text	
Firstname	Text	
Title	Text	
Street	Text	
Town	Text	
County	Text	
Post Code	Text	
Telephone No	Text	
Occupation	Text	
Date of Birth	Date/Time	
Date of Joining	Date/Time	
Date of Last Renewal	Date/Time	
Sporting Interests	Memo	
Smoker	Yes/No	
Sex	Yes/No	

1 Enter **Membership No** for the first field name.	Do not type a full stop after **No** because these are not allowed in field names. For more information on field names refer to the section on *Naming Fields*, below.

2 Press *Enter* to move to the Data Type column and click on the [list] button, which displays the following list box.

⊞ Table1 : Table	
Field Name	**Data Type**
▶ Membership No	Text ▼
	Text
	Memo
	Number
	Date/Time
	Currency
	AutoNumber
	Yes/No
	OLE Object
	Lookup Wizard...

3 Click on the data type AutoNumber. Press *Enter* and you will be in the description field. Key in the description as shown in the table.

4 Press *Enter* to move to the next field.	See below for details of moving around the table design window.
5 Continue to enter the definitions for the fields as detailed in the table. Where there is no description press *Enter* to take you to the next field name.	The table will be revisited later to set individual field properties.
6 The next stage is to define the primary key. Click on the row selector(see below) for Membership No and click on the [Primary Key] button [🔑] on the toolbar	Primary keys will be discussed in more detail later.

You will save this table definition in Task 4.

Moving around the table design window

Through the table design window you can enter the field name, the data type and a description of each field (the description is optional) into the grid in the upper part of the window. To move between cells you have a choice of pressing either *Enter*, *TAB* or the right arrow key or clicking in the required cell in the grid.

Row selector symbols

Along the left-hand edge of the grid you will see the row selector symbols. By clicking in the row selector box you can select an entire row.

Row	Selector symbol
Current row	
Primary key field	

Naming fields

Fields need names, lengths and data types to be defined. Many database products limit you to about 10 characters for a field name, which means that names often need to be abbreviated. Also, the use of spaces in a field name is not usually allowed. However, *Access allows field names to be up to 64 characters long with spaces.* Field names should be meaningful so that the data is easier to work with. Some characters are not allowed in field names: full stops (.), exclamation marks (!), and square brackets ([]). You cannot give the same name to more than one field. Why not?

The length of a field may be predetermined according to the data type of that particular field. If the field is of a date type then it will have a standard length. Other data types such as text and number can have their lengths defined. If a text field is being used to hold the title of a song, for example, then you will need to estimate the length of the longest song title and set the size of the field accordingly.

Adding a field description

A description for a field may be added into the description cell in the table's design view, for any field. The maximum length for the description is 255 characters. It is not necessary to enter a description but it can be useful to provide additional information about a particular field.

Correcting mistakes in a field name or description

Point and click in the cell containing the mistake. Correct the mistake in the normal fashion by inserting or deleting text at the insertion point. Click back in the current cell to continue working.

Correcting mistakes in the data type

Click on the data type cell concerned. Open the list box and select the correct data type.

Creating a primary key

The primary key is a field or combination of fields that uniquely identifies each record in a table. As the main index for the table, it is used to associate data between tables. Although it is not required, a primary key is highly recommended. All of the tables used in our system will have a primary key defined. It speeds data retrieval and enables you to define default relationships between tables. In FIGURE 2.1 the primary field keys are shown in bold italics. If the **Membership** table is considered, then the membership number is the primary key; each record has a different number because every member's number will be different.

 If the table does not include an obvious primary key field, you can have Microsoft Access set up a field that assigns a unique number to each record. This automatically numbers each record uniquely. See Unit 5 for more discussion of primary keys.

Task 3: Setting or changing the primary key

This is an optional task, which you may find useful to try on tables that you additionally create with Access.

To set or change the primary key:

1	In the table's design view, select the field or fields you want to define as the primary key.	To select one field, click the row selector. To select multiple fields, hold down down the *Ctrl* key, and click the row selectors for each field.
2	Click on the **Primary key** button 🔑 on the toolbar, or choose **Edit-Primary Key**.	Microsoft Access places the primary key icon in the row selector column.

To have Access define the primary key:

3	With the table's design view displayed, save the table without specifying a primary key.	Access asks if you want it to create a primary key field.
4	Choose Yes	Access creates a field in your table called **ID** with the AutoNumber data type.

Saving the table definition

Once the structure of the table has been designed, it needs to be saved. Access uses this information to set up templates through which you enter data into the table.

 The table is saved as part of the database file and its name distinguishes it from other tables in the database file. There may be more than one table in a database file and Access allows more freedom for naming tables. You will also find this true for naming queries, forms, reports and macros, as all of these are stored in one database file. Make use of this freedom to give meaningful names to tables because they will be used later in queries, forms and reports, and it is important to be able to recognise the name of the table you require.

Task 4: Saving the table definition

Continuing from Task 2:

1   Choose **File-Save**.

2   In the **Save As** dialog box, type the name *Membership* in the **Table Name** box and click on **OK** .

3   Close the table using **File-Close** (shortcut key *Ctrl-w*).

Note that the name you choose may be 255 characters long and may contain any alphanumeric text.

Closing and opening the table

To close a table, either:

1 Double-click on the table's control menu button, or

2 Choose **File-Close**.

You can open an existing table in either design view or datasheet view. So far we have only considered the design view of a table.

To open a table in design view:

1 In the Database window, click on the **Table** 'tab'.

2 Select the table you want to open, and then click on the **Design** button.

Defining field properties

What you will learn in this unit

Once a database table has been created, the fields named and the type of data to be stored in the field chosen, further refinements to fields may be made by setting field properties. At the end of this unit you should be able to:

■ define field properties.

Defining field properties

You may have noticed that once you start to enter the field definitions, field name, data type and description, then the field properties are displayed in the lower left-hand section of the design window (FIGURE 4.1). You have defined the basic data type for each field, and by setting the field properties you can specify the data type in more detail. For example, if the data type is text you can define the length of the field.

General	Lookup	
Field Size	10	
Format		
Input Mask		
Caption		
Default Value		
Validation Rule		
Validation Text		
Required	No	
Allow Zero Length	No	
Indexed	No	

FIGURE 4.1

In the Field Properties section, you can set properties for individual fields. The available options depend on the data type you define for the field. In the lower right-hand section of the window a description of the current column or field property is displayed.

The set of properties for each field specifies how you want data stored, handled and displayed. The properties you can set for each field are determined by the data type you select for the field.

Setting a field property

In the table's Design view, select the field whose properties you want to set. Next, click the property you want to set in the bottom part of the window. Then set the property, as explained in the following table.

Property	Description
Field Size	Maximum length of the text field or type of number
Format	How data is displayed; use predefined formats or customise your own
Input Mask	Data entry pattern
Caption	Default field label in a form or report
Default Value	Value entered in a field when records are created
Validation Rule	Expression that defines data entry rules
Validation Text	Text for invalid data
Required	Whether or not an entry must be made
Allow Zero Length	Allows you to store a zero length string ("") to indicate data that exists but is unknown.
Indexed	Single-field indexes to speed searches

Field size

This property sets the maximum size of data that can be stored in a field. If the Data Type property is set to Text, enter a number less than 255. This number should be chosen by considering the length of the longest text data that is to be entered into the field. The default setting is 50.

If the Data Type property is set to Number, the Field Size property settings and their values are related in the following way:

Setting	Description
Byte	Stores whole numbers with values between 0 and 255. Occupies 1 byte.
Integer	Stores whole numbers with values between –32,768 and 32,767. Occupies 2 bytes.
Long Integer (default)	Stores numbers from -2,147,483,648 to 2,147,483,647 (no fractions). Occupies 4 bytes.
Single	Stores numbers with six digits of precision, from –3.402823E38 to 3.402823E38. Occupies 4 bytes.
Double	Stores numbers with ten digits of precision, from –1.79769313486232E308 to 1.79769313486232E308. Occupies 8 bytes.

Defaults

Access will assign default values to the fields in your table. These default values are automatically entered in the field when a new record is created. These are values that are usually appropriate for the addition of new records to a table. The default value for **Number**, **Currency** and **Yes/No** fields is zero (in the case of **Yes/No** fields, zero means No). **Text**, **Memo** and **Date** fields are empty by default. You can save time by specifying your own default values for fields.

You can specify a default field using text or an expression. For example, in an address table you might set the default for the **Town** field to London, if the majority of records are London addresses. When users add records to the table, they can either accept this value or enter the name of a different town or city. If, for example, an **Orders** table contains the field **Order Date** then the expression *=Date()* can be used to put the current date into this field.

Validation

The data entered into tables must be accurate if the database is to be valuable to the person or organisation that it serves. However, even the most experienced data entry operator can make mistakes. To try to detect mistakes you can test the data entered by creating validation rules. These are simple tests, which are entered as short expressions into the Validation Rule text box.

If the data entered does not conform to your validation rule, a message box will be displayed to inform the operator that the data is incorrect. The message in the message box is defined by the text that you put in the Validation Text text box. The maximum length for both the Validation Rule and the Validation Text boxes is 255 characters. If data in a record is amended then the validation will still be performed. If no validation rule for a field has been entered, then no validation will be performed on that field.

Examples of expressions that can be used are often concerned with numeric fields, for example a credit limit that cannot be greater than a certain value. Fields with other data types may also be validated, for example a date may only be entered in a certain time period, or a code can be checked to see if it is a correct department code.

Required entry

By setting the required property of a field to Yes you will need to make an entry in that particular field for every record. Where it is not necessary to have an entry then this property can be left as its default value. In the **Membership** table the **Category No** field has been defined as required; thus, a member cannot be enrolled without being given a category of membership. As you create the **Membership** table in the following task, consider which fields in this table are required entry and set this property.

Task 1: Defining field properties

So far we have not changed any of the field properties. In this task the field properties of the **Membership** table will be defined. You should be able to complete this exercise by following the immediate instructions, but additional notes are also given in the activities described in the following few pages, which you may wish to consult. First, open the **Membership** table in design view

1. From the **Database Window**, click on **Membership** and click on the **Design** button.

2. Select the field **Category No**.

   This field has a data type of Number and the field properties are preset as Field Size – Long Integer, Decimal Places – Auto, Default Value – 0, Required – No and Indexed – No. In this field the data that will be entered is a number between 1 and 6 inclusive, as there are 6 categories. Refer to the section entitled *Field size* to see a list of the different number properties that are available. The Byte number type allows whole numbers up to 255 so it is a good choice for the number property of the **Category No** field.

3. Click in the **Field Size** box, open its associated list and select Byte.

   There are only six categories so a validation rule can be created.

4. Click in the **Validation Rule** box and key in **<=6**; key in the text **Please enter a category number between 1 and 6** in the **Validation Text** box.

5. To prevent a number less than 1 being entered, modify the validation rule to read <=6 And >0.

6. Open the **Required list** box and select Yes.

   It is necessary for there to be an entry in this field.

7. Select the field **Lastname**.

8. Click in the **Field Size** box, delete the default size of 50 and replace it with 25

9   Alter the sizes of the other text
    fields as follows:

Firstname	30
Title	10
Street	30
Town	25
County	20
Post Code	10
Telephone No	12

10 Select the **Town** field again and in
   the **Default Value** box type ***Chelmer***.

11 Select the **County** field and put
   Cheshire into its **Default Value** box.
   Why do think these defaults are set?
   Refer to the section on defaults, above.

12 Select the **Date of Birth** field and   Alternatively, select **Short Date** from
   in the **Format** box key the format   the drop-down list of the **Format** box.
   d/m/yy (to suppress leading zeros
   on day and month) or ***dd/mm/yy***
   (to display leading zeros). Repeat
   this for the two other date fields.

13 Select the **Smoker** field and in the   Note it is important to put the first
   Format box replace Yes/No with the   semi-colon.
   format ;*"Smoker";"Non-Smoker"*
   which will display Smoker for Yes
   and Non-Smoker for No.

14 Click on the **Lookup** tab and then   This is so the defined formats will be
   click on the *Display control down*   displayed.
   arrow. Select **Text** Box. Click on the
   General tab.

15 Select the **Sex** field and in the **Format** box replace Yes/No with the format
   ;*"Male";"Female"* which will display Male for Yes and Female for No. Set the
   Display Control to **Text** Box as for the **Smoker** field.

16 Save the changes using **File-Save** and close the table using **File-Close**.

Creating custom display formats

Custom formats will display the data in the format that is specified regardless of the
format in which it is entered. For example, a display format can be created which
will show all telephone numbers using a particular format, e.g. (01777) 565656 or
01777-565656. A custom format is created from an image of the format. To design

25

the image a special set of characters known as *placeholders* are used. To illustrate the creation of a custom format some examples are shown in the following table:

Numeric format	The # indicates the place for a digit, but if the place is not used then leading and trailing zeros are not shown. The 0 indicates a place for a digit; if the place is not used then a 0 is shown. The comma may be used as a thousands separator.
##,###.00	Examples: 56.98 6.90 5,890.07 100.00
#0.000	Examples: 12.456 0.020
Date	The days placeholder is d. d displays 1, dd 01, ddd Mon, and dddd Monday. The months placeholder is m. m displays 1, mm 01, mmm Jan, and mmmm January. The years placeholder is y. yy displays 97, yyyy 1997.
	The / or - separates the day, month and year.
dddd d mmmm yyyy	Example: Tuesday 25 March 1997
dd/mm/yy	26/06/97
d-m-yy	2-5-97 (this format does not display leading zeros).
Time	The hours placeholder is h. h displays 3, hh 03. The minutes placeholder is m. m displays 6, mm 06. The seconds placeholder is s. s displays 7, ss 07.
	The colon separates hours, minutes and seconds. AM/PM or am/pm display time in 12- or 24-hour format, respectively.
h:mm AM/PM	Example: 6:34 PM
hh:mm:ss	Example: 11:09:57
Text	@ indicates that a character is required in the particular position.
>	Changes all text in the field to uppercase.
<	Changes all text in the field to lowercase.
(@@@@) @@@@@@	Example: (0777) 565656
Yes/No	Example: ;"Male";"Female"
	Displays Male for true and Female for false.

Task 2: Customising a field format

1 Open the **Chelmer** database and open the **Membership** table in design view.

2 Select the **Post Code** field and put **>** in the Format property.

3 Save and close the table using **File-Save** followed by **File-Close**.

Creating input masks

Data entry can be made simpler by creating an input mask, which is a particular format or pattern in which the data is entered. An input mask is only suitable where all of the data for that particular field has the same pattern, for example stock numbers such as ABM-372-4590-C. To illustrate the creation of an input mask some examples are shown in the following table:

Input mask	Sample values
\ABM-000-0000->L	ABM-372-4590-C
0000-000000	0777-567890
>L<??????????????????	Jackson

A mask is created using special mask symbols, which are described in the following table:

Mask character	Indicates ...
0	A number (digit) must be entered
9	A digit may be entered
#	A digit, + or - sign, or space may be entered
L	A letter must be entered
?	A letter may be entered
A	A letter or digit must be entered
a	A letter or digit may be entered
&	Any character or space must be entered
C	Any character or space may be entered
. , : ; - /	Decimal point, thousands, date and time separators
<	Characters to the right are converted to lower case
>	Characters to the right are converted to upper case
\	The character following is *not* to be interpreted as a mask character

Task 3: Setting an input mask

Revisit the properties of the **Lastname** field and set the mask using the third example illustrated above. Check that you use the correct number of question marks, i.e. 24, which is one less than the field width of 25.

Creating table indexes

What you will learn in this unit

Fields in a database table may be indexed, which can speed up retrieval of records. This unit explains the function of indexes and indicates how to select indexes. It is important to maintain documentation concerning the fields and the properties chosen for them. A standard way to do this is by printing a table definition using the Documentor facility provided with Access. At the end of this unit you should be able to:

■ create table indexes

■ print a table definition.

Creating table indexes

What is an index? You are probably familiar with the index at the back of a book, which helps you to find a particular topic quickly. A table index works in a similar fashion, enabling Access to locate a particular record without having to search through all of the records from the first until it locates the one you want. When you enter data into a table the records are in chronological order according to when you entered them; in other words, they are in no particular order.

A useful order for the table to be in would be that of the primary key. The primary key uniquely defines one record from another, so this is a logical order for the records to be in. If the records are not physically in primary key order then Access does not physically rearrange them; rather, it creates an index which it uses to locate the records in that particular order.

When a primary key is defined the indexed property is automatically set to Yes (No Duplicates). No duplicates means that Access expects this field in each record to be unique, which it should be if it is a primary key field.

Indexes on other fields may be defined because an index helps Access to find specific records faster. For example, an index on surname and forename together is useful if the Membership table is often searched using the member's name. Another index could be set on the Date of Renewal field, useful when the table is used to provide projected cash flow of membership fees.

 Do not index every field in your table because this slows record updating; each time a record is added the indexes need to be modified to account for the new record. The fields you should choose for indexing are ones that are used repeatedly to search for data.

You can create indexes based on a single field or on multiple fields. For example, you can index just on a surname name field or on both surname and forename fields. An index on surnames will not distinguish between Liam Locker and Alison Locker but an index on the multiple fields surname and forename will. Another example is a date and time in the **Booking** table. Multiple-field indexes enable you to distinguish records in which the first field may have the same value. Instead of finding nine booking records for Monday, you can find one record for Monday at 14:00.

Creating a single-field index

In the table's Design view, select the field you want to index. In the Indexed property box at the bottom of the window, choose Yes (Duplicates OK) or Yes (No Duplicates). Choose the Yes (No Duplicates) option to ensure that no two records have the same data in this field.

Creating a multiple-field index

In the Design view of the table, choose **View-Indexes** or click on the **Indexes** button ▦ on the toolbar. Access displays the **Indexes** dialog box.

In the **Index Name** column enter the name of the index. In the **Field Name** column open the list box and select the field you require; set the sort order in the **Sort Order** column.

In the next row select the next field name of the multiple index and set its sort order. By leaving the Index name blank, up to nine subsequent rows may be used to create a multiple field index, with each field having its own sort order defined. Note that fields should be listed in order of priority.

Task 1: Setting indexes

1   Open the **Membership** table in
     Design view.

2   Select the **Category No** field and
     choose Yes (Duplicates OK).

3   Repeat for **Date of Birth** and **Date**   Why can't Yes (No Duplicates) be chosen?
     of Joining, choosing Yes (Duplicates
     OK) for the indexed property.

4   Save these table design modifications
     using **File-Save**.

5 Display the **Indexes** dialog box. In
the **Index Name** column enter the
name *Member.* List the fields **Lastname**
and **Firstname** as illustrated below:

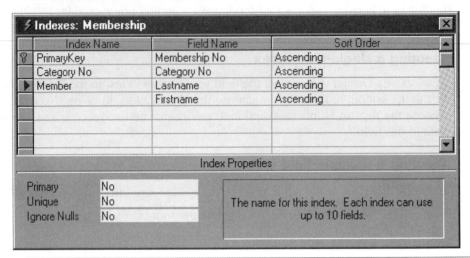

Making a printed copy of the table design

Access allows you to view and print the design characteristics (definition) of your
tables, forms, queries and reports. To make a printed copy of the table design:

1 Choose **Tools-Analyze**, and then click **Documentor**. Note: you may need to install
the Access analysing tools; follow the instructions given in the error message.

2 In the **Object Type** box, enter the type of database object you want to view or
print. In this case choose Tables.

3 In the **Objects** box, click on the name of the table for which definitions are
required.

4 Click **Options** to specify which features of the selected object you want to print,
and then click on **OK**.

5 You might want to check the length of your definitions in the Print Preview
window, because some definitions, particularly those for forms and reports, can be
many pages long.

6 To print the definition, click on the **Print** button on the toolbar.

Before such tools were available, database designers created another table as a
means of storing table definitions, i.e. a data dictionary. This required more work but
gave a more complete perspective and a chance to revise the work already done.
Each data element in the database system had an entry in a dictionary table.

Task 2: Printing the Membership table definition

1 Display the Database window,
and follow steps 1 to 3 above.

2 Choose the **Membership** table and
click on **Options**. Set the following
options:

3 Include for Table: Properties

4 Include for Fields: Names, Data
Types, and Sizes

5 Include for Indexes: Names
and Fields

6 Click on **OK** to exit the Print
Table Definition window, then
on OK again.

Be prepared that Access may take a little
time to compile the definition.

7 Preview and print the table definition.

Entering and editing data

What you will learn in this unit

In this unit you will see how to:

■ display a table's datasheet and use it to enter data

■ make a backup copy of your table.

Entering data

The next stage is to enter data into the tables. Up until now the table has only been opened in Design view. To enter data a table needs to be opened in the Datasheet view.

Opening a table in Datasheet view

In the Database window, click the **Table** tab. Double-click the table name or select the table, and choose the **Open** button. The table will open in datasheet view.

Once a table is open it is possible to switch from the Datasheet view to the Design view and vice versa. If you make changes to the design you will be asked to save them if you switch back to the Datasheet view. There is a button on the toolbar for switching between the views:

When in Design view	*When in Datasheet view*

 button   **Design view** button

In the Datasheet view the headings of the columns are the field names that you designed previously. Each row in the datasheet is a record and as you complete each record it is automatically saved into the table.

Task 1: Membership data

1 Open the **Membership** table in Datasheet view.

Notice that there are some fields already filled in; these are the default values. A default value can be accepted or it can be overridden.

2　Do not enter a value into the membership number but press *Enter* to move to the next field.

This is a counter field; if you do try to enter data into it the entry will not be accepted. When you press *Enter* after entering data into the last field of the first record, Access saves the record. Notice what appears in the membership number field. Let Access number all of the membership number fields.

3　Enter the data for the **Membership** table as shown in Quick Reference 2.

4　After entering the data for each field move to the next by pressing *Enter*, *Tab* or the right arrow key. When entering the data for the logical fields enter either **Yes** or **No** and the appropriate word as defined by the format will appear, e.g. Male or Female. Also, while entering the data test the validation rules, both those that Access applies and those that have been defined. Try the following:

5　Entering text into a date-type field.

Access expects the correct data type.

6　Entering a Category No greater than 6.

This will test the validation rule set up in the field properties for Category No.

7　Skip fields that are blank.

Validation, skipping fields and using **Undo** are described below.

Validation

Data is validated as it is entered. If it does not conform to the data type set for that field an error message will be generated. If the data entered breaks the validation rule that has been set as a property for that field, then if there is validation text, this appears as the error message.

Skipping fields, null values

Sometimes not all of the data for a record is available; for example, the telephone number may be missing. To skip a field simply press *Enter* or *Tab* to take you to the next field. It is acceptable to skip fields where the data is not vital, but for data such as the membership number it is not acceptable. Access automatically enters a membership number because the field was defined with an AutoNumber data type.

Where a field is left without an entry it is said to be Null, i.e. there is nothing there.

If you perform mathematical calculations on numeric fields, then Access ignores fields containing Nulls. This can lead to errors in statistical analysis; for example, you will meet a query in Unit 13 that calculates the average age of the members. There are 20 member records; if a 21st record is added where there is no entry in the **Date of Birth** field, from which age is calculated, then the average of the 20 known ages will be calculated. However, if a count of members is requested based on Membership No then the result would be 21. If you intend to use a numeric field for calculation then it is good practice to try to ensure that each record has an entry in that field.

Zero length strings

Nulls indicate that data may exist but is not known. To enter a null leave a field's Required property as No and leave the field blank. A zero length string can be used to indicate that there is no data for the field in that record; for example, a company without a fax machine does not have a fax number. To enter a zero length string check that the Allow Zero Length property is set to Yes. In the datasheet, type two double quotation marks without a space between them, i.e. "". Nulls and zero length strings may be distinguished when searching the data table.

Using undo

Should you do anything wrong, or if something unexpected happens, always try **Edit-Undo** or click on the **Undo** button 🔁 before doing anything else.

Editing data

Once the records have been entered into a table, this data is available to be used, as is evident in the following sessions. However, the data in the datasheet can be viewed and if mistakes are spotted these can be rectified.

Moving between records

By using either **Edit-Go To**, the *up* and *down* arrow keys, the *page up* and *page down* keys or the vertical scroll bar, you can move between records in the datasheet. However, the most efficient way to move between records in large databases is with the navigation buttons in the lower-left corner of the window.

Access record indicators

In the status bar of the datasheet window are the Access record indicators (FIGURE 6.1). These are record movement buttons and the record number of the currently selected record.

FIGURE 6.1

To move to ...	Click
First record	⏮
Last record	⏭
Previous record	◀
Next record	▶
New record	▶✳
Specific record	Click in the record counter box [1]

(or press *F5*), type the record number you want, and then press *Enter*.

Selecting data

Various parts of the datasheet can be selected. When an area is selected it appears in inverse colour, so if text is normally black on white, then selected text is white on black.

To select ...	...do this
■ To select a single field	move the pointer to the left-hand side of a cell, so that it changes shape into a white cross, and click.
■ To select a word in a field	double-click on the word.
■ To select a record	click in the record selector at the left edge of the record, or choose **Edit-Select Record**.
■ To select more than one record	click and drag in the record selector edge for the required number of records.
■ To select a field column	click on the column heading (the field name at the top of the column).
■ To select several field columns	click on the first column heading required for the selection and drag to the last.

Moving and copying fields

A field may be moved by selecting it, using **Edit-Cut**, clicking in the cell where the field is to be moved to and using **Edit-Paste**.

A field may be copied, by selecting it, using **Edit-Copy**, clicking in the cell where the copy is required and using **Edit-Paste**. Buttons are also available, i.e. **Cut** , **Copy**

and **Paste** : ✂ 🗐 📋

Hiding and showing columns

If there are a lot of fields in a table as is the case with the **Membership** table then columns may be hidden. By using the Show command the columns may be re-displayed. To hide a column in a datasheet:

1 Click on the column selector at the top of the column. More than one column may be selected for hiding.

2 Choose **Format-Hide Columns**.

To re-display the columns:

3 Choose **Format-Unhide Columns**.

4 In the dialog box select the column(s) to be unhidden and click on Close .

Moving and copying records

You can copy a complete table or some records of a table to the clipboard. Records may be moved and copied using **Edit-Cut/Copy** and **Edit-Paste**. Generally moving is not an operation you would need to carry out within the same table because the records can be displayed in any order chosen. Moving and also copying can be carried out between databases providing the table structures are similar. Importing and exporting data is considered in more detail in Units 35 to 38.

One instance where copying is useful is for making a backup of a table. Should you decide to revise the data types of fields in a table then it is advisable to make a backup of the table first in case mistakes are made, which could result in the loss of data.

Task 2: Backing up a table

In this task a backup of the **Membership** table will be made.

1 Click on the Table tab in the **Database window**.

2 Select the **Membership** table and choose **Edit-Copy**.

3 Next create a database to hold the backup by choosing **File-New Database**, selecting the folder in which the backup file is to be stored, typing **CHELMER BACKUP** in the **File name** box and clicking on the Create button.   This database is now active.

4 Choose **Edit-Paste** and in the **Table Name** box of the **Paste Table As** dialog box type ***Membership Backup***.

5 Check that the default option **Structure and Data** is selected before clicking on **OK** .

6 Use **File-Close** to close the backup database.

If this backup is needed to restore a damaged file then open the backup database, select and copy the table, open the normal database (use **File-Open Database**) and paste as described above.

Managing data

What you will learn in this unit

In this unit you will see how to:

- delete data
- use find and replace to edit data
- print the data in your table.

Deleting records

 You can delete a record from a table using a datasheet or a form. (You will meet forms in Unit 14). Here you see how to delete records using a datasheet.

Deleting a record

1 Select the record or records you wish to delete.

2 Press the *Delete* key (or choose **Edit-Delete** from the menu).

3 Access prompts you to confirm the deletion. Choose **Yes** to delete the record or **No** to retain it.

Finding and replacing

To find a particular field:

1 If you wish to find a particular entry in a certain field make that field current by clicking in that column.

2 Choose either **Edit-Find** or click on the **Find** button on the toolbar.

FIGURE 7.1

3 Key the string (set of characters) you wish to find into the **Find What** text box.

4 In the **Search** box choose between **Up**, **Down** or **All**.

5 In the **Match** box select whether your string should match the whole field, any part of the field or the start of the field.

6 In the **Match Case** check box you may choose between making your search case sensitive or not.

7 In the **Search Fields As Formatted** check box you may choose between finding a field as, say, a number 28/3/96 or as it is formatted 28-Mar-96.

8 In the **Search Only Current Field** check box you may choose between limiting your search to the current field or including all fields.

9 To start the search click on either **Find Next** , which will search from your current position in the direction you have chosen, or **Find First** , which will find the first occurrence in the field or table. Each time a match is found it is highlighted. If either the top or the bottom of the table is reached Access displays a message asking whether you would like to continue the search from the bottom or the top of the table.

10 When you have found the desired field click on **Close** .

To replace a particular field, select **Edit-Replace**. The steps are the same as for finding a field, except that in the dialog box there is an additional text box, **Replace With**, into which the replacement string is entered. Strings can be replaced according to which button is clicked:

■ **Find Next** : finds and highlights but does not replace. Use when you do not want to replace.

■ **Replace** : replaces the highlighted string and finds the next occurrence of the Find What string.

■ **Replace All** : replaces all occurrences of the string without stopping.

■ **Close** : closes the dialog box

Task 1: Editing data

In this task we experiment with finding and replacing data.

1 Open the **Membership** table in Datasheet view. Move to the end of the table.

2 Add another record, Category 3. Move to record 9, select the **Lastname** field and copy it.

3 Move back to the **Lastname** field of the new record and use **Edit-Paste**. Finish the record as shown in the table below:

Firstname	Title	Street	Town	County	Post Code
Frances	Miss	70 Meir View	Chelmer	Cheshire	CH2 7BZ

Date of Birth	Date of Joining	Date of Last Renewal	Sporting interests	Smoker	Sex
5/5/82	1/3/95	1/3/96	Swimming, Judo	No	No

4   Go to the first record. Click in the **Telephone No** field.

5   Choose **Edit-Find** or click on the ▮Find▮ button on the toolbar.

6   Key *01778* into the **Find What** box and select **Start of field**.

7   Click on the ▮Find First▮ button. This should highlight the first occurrence. If the **Find in field** dialog box is in the way, drag it out of the way.

8   Click on the ▮Find Next▮ button to find other matches. Close the **Find in field** dialog box.

9   Move to the top of the table again and click in the **Telephone No** field. Choose **Edit-Replace** and key *01777* into the **Find What** box and *01779* into the **Replace With** box.

The current field should be selected to search in and the **Match Whole Field** check box should not be checked, as shown below:

10 Click on the ▮Replace All▮ button.

11 Answer Yes to continue but note that at this point you could abandon the operation.

12 Now replace all 01779 codes with *01777*.

13 Select the last record, which you have just created, and delete it.

Customising the datasheet layout

Adjusting column widths

To improve the datasheet display, it is possible to alter the widths of the columns. Usually columns are made smaller, because field widths often err on the large side, and this is easily achieved, especially if you are familiar with Windows applications.

To alter a column width:

1 Move the pointer to the field name row (at the top of the table).

2 Move the pointer to the dividing line between the column you wish to change and the column to the right. It should change shape to a ⟷ .

3 Click and drag the column to the desired width.

Adjusting row heights

Another way in which more fields can be displayed across the screen is by making the row height larger. Instead of widening a column to see all of the data in a field, if the row height is increased the data in the field will wrap. To alter a row height:

1 Move the pointer to the row selector (at the left edge of the table).

2 Move the pointer to the dividing line between the row you wish to change and the row below. It should change shape to a ⤒ .

3 Click and drag the row to the desired height. Note that all rows take on the new height.

Changing the font used in the datasheet

Choose **Format-Font** and select the required font and size from the **Font** dialog box.

Changing and reorganising fields

 You may find it necessary to change a field data type as the design of your database develops or if you import data into it. Units 35 and 36 deal with importing data. Before you make any changes to field data types make a backup copy of the table in case you accidentally lose data because your changes were too great.

Before you make changes consider the following implications.

 ■ Numeric fields: changing from one data type to another that can hold a larger number is generally safe, for example changing a data type of Byte to Integer (refer to Unit 4 for definitions of field size). If, on the other hand, you change to a data type that holds a smaller number, for example from Double to Integer, then your data will be truncated, in this case by losing the decimal part of the number. Truncation means reducing the number of digits in a number to fit the new field size property that you choose. Note: you cannot convert any type of field into a Counter (AutoNumber) type field as Access provides automatic numbering in this field type.

- Text fields: the field size of text fields may be altered, but if the alteration is to make the field size smaller, text may be truncated. Text fields may be converted to Memo fields, but if a Memo field is converted to a text field it will be truncated to 255 characters.

- Conversion between data types: it is possible to convert a field from one data type to another.

- Primary key or fields used in relationships: you cannot change the data type or field size property of these fields.

To change a field data type, make a backup copy of your table, display the design view of your table and make the necessary alterations.

Reorganising fields

If you consider that the order in which the fields are shown in the datasheet needs to be rearranged, then this can easily be achieved using a drag and drop method. First select the field column you wish to move, move the pointer over the selection so that it changes shape to a left-pointing arrow, click (the pointer changes shape to drag and drop) and drag the column to a new position. A darker column dividing line will indicate where the field will go when the mouse button is released.

When you close the table you can choose whether or not to make the rearrangement permanent by selecting Yes or No in the **Save Changes** message box.

Displaying data in sorted order

The data displayed in a datasheet will be displayed in natural order, that is in the order in which the records were entered. This may not be the order in which you would like to see them. You can control the order of the records using the

Sort Ascending and **Sort Descending** buttons on the toolbar.

To change the displayed order of the records using one field:

1 Select a column by which you wish to sort (click on the field name at the top of the column).

2 Click on either the **Sort Ascending** or **Sort Descending** button.

To change the displayed order of the records using more than one field:

1 Select the columns by which you wish to sort (click on the field name at the top of the first column and drag to the last column). Sorting columns must be next to one another, with the highest priority being assigned to the leftmost column. If necessary rearrange the columns in the datasheet.

2 Click on either the **Sort Ascending** or **Sort Descending** button.

Task 2: Customising the membership datasheet

The aim of this task is to see how columns of data may be rearranged, and also how to adjust their width.

1 Display the **Membership** datasheet.

2 Adjust the widths of the columns to accommodate the data displayed.

3 Select the **Sporting Interests** column and drag it to between the **Occupation** and the **Date of Birth** columns.

4 Close the table without making the rearrangement permanent by choosing No in the Save Changes message box when closing the table.

Task 3: Displaying records in sorted order

In this task the records in the **Membership** table will be viewed in different orders.

1 Open the **Membership** table in datasheet view.

2 Select the **Lastname** column and click on the Sort Ascending button. Click on the Sort Descending button.

3 Try this for other fields in the table.

4 Select the **Category No** and **Lastname** columns together and click on the Sort Ascending button. Note the effect.

5 Drag the **Town** column so it is to the right of the **Category No** column, select these two columns, and click on the Sort Ascending button.

6 Drag the **Town** column so it is to the left of the **Category No** column, select these two columns, and click on the Sort Ascending button.

Note the difference between these last two sorts.

7 Close the **Membership** table without saving the layout changes.

Printing a table

You can print a table from its datasheet. Access prints a datasheet as it appears on the screen. For large datasheets, Microsoft Access prints from left to right and then from top to bottom. For example, if your datasheet is three pages wide and two pages long, Microsoft Access prints the top three pages first, then the bottom three pages. You should preview your datasheet before printing by choosing **File-Print Preview** or clicking on the **Print Preview** button 🔍 on the toolbar.

If you need to set up your printer, choose the **Setup** button in the **Print** dialog box.

Printing a table datasheet

■ Display the table datasheet.

■ If you intend to print selected records, select those records. To print all of the records, select nothing.

■ Choose **File-Print Preview**, and if the preview is satisfactory choose **File-Print** to display the **Print** dialog box.

■ Under **Print Range**, choose one of the following: **All**, to print all the records in the table; **Pages**, to print specific pages from your table; or **Selected Records**, to print the records of your choice. If you select **Pages**, specify the page numbers of the first and last pages you want to print.

■ Set other **Print** dialog box options if necessary.

■ Choose **OK** .

Task 4: Printing the membership table

1   Display the **Membership** table datasheet.

2   Choose **File-Print Preview**, and then select **File-Print** to display the **Print** dialog box.

3   Under **Print Range** select **All** and click on **OK** .

4   Close the table.

Relationships between tables

What you will learn in this unit

If you wish to use only one table in your database you may omit this unit. You will find that you can complete most of Units 10 to 31 as many exercises are based on the **Membership** table. You should then return to this activity before moving on to Unit 32. In this unit you will be introduced to the concept of the relationship between tables, and you will see how to:

■ define and create relationships between tables

■ apply referential integrity.

Defining relationships between tables

The relationships between the tables are shown in FIGURE 8.1. Relationships are made between a field in one table and a field in another table. Relationships fall into three types:

■ one-to-one relationships

■ one-to-many relationships

■ many-to-many relationships.

A one-to-one relationship between two tables means that for a particular field in one table there is only one matching record in the other table and vice versa. A one-to-many relationship means that for one field in one table there are lots of matching records in the other table. A many-to-many relationship means that for one field in one table there are lots of matching records in the other table and vice versa.

The commonest type of relationship is that of one-to-many and it is the only type used in our system. Consider the relationship between a member and that member's booking. A member may make no bookings, one booking or several bookings. So one member can make several bookings, a one-to-many relationship, i.e. there is only one record with that person's membership number in the **Membership** table, yet there can be several records with that person's membership number in the bookings table.

However, in our database these relationships do not yet exist because they have not been defined. You need to set up these relationships. The relationships can be set up before any actual data is entered into any of the tables. Before any relationships between tables can be defined the tables must be closed. It is important that when a link is make between a field in one table and a field in another table, the two fields have the same data type.

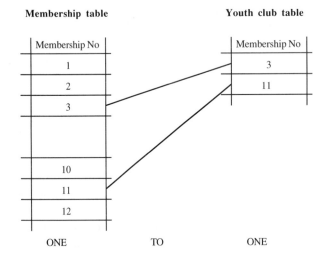

Membership table

Bookings table

Membership No
1
2
3

Membership No
4
1
6
8
1
17
3

ONE   TO   MANY

Membership table

Youth club table

Membership No
1
2
3
10
11
12

Membership No
3
11

ONE   TO   ONE

FIGURE 8.1

Referential integrity

When a relationship is created between two tables Access allows the choice of whether or not to enforce referential integrity. If the relationship between the **Membership** and the **Bookings** table is considered, then what is to stop a membership number being entered into the **Bookings** table which does not exist in the **Membership** table? By enforcing referential integrity Access will check the membership number entered into the **Bookings** table against the membership numbers in the **Membership** table and will prevent non-existent membership numbers being entered.

Task 1: Creating relationships

As yet, only one table has been created in the **Chelmer** database. Before relationships can be defined the other tables in the database need to be defined. In this Task the **Bookings** table will be defined.

1 To create a **Bookings** table, click on the New button in the **Database** window to open the table design window (you may wish to refer back to Units 3 and 4). Define the field types as shown.

2 Define **Booking No** as the primary key. Save the table as **Bookings.**

Bookings table

Field name	Data type	Description
Booking No	Auto Number	
Room/Hall/Court	Text	
Member/Class	Yes/No	
Membership No	Number	
Class No	Number	
Date	Date/Time	
Time	Date/Time	

3 Amend the field properties as shown below. Save and close the table.

Bookings table

Field	Property	Setting
Room/Hall/Court	Field Size	20
	Required	Yes
Member/Class	Format	;"Member";"Class"
	Required	Yes
Membership No	Field Size	Long Integer
	Default value	=Null
Class No	Field Size	Long Integer
	Default value	=Null
Date	Format	d/m/yy
	Required	Yes
Time	Format	Short time
	Required	Yes

4 Make sure that both the tables are closed, i.e. just the **Database window** is left open.

Now the relationship between **Membership No** in the **Membership** table and **Membership No** in the **Bookings** table can be created. The data type of the **Membership No (Bookings)** is a long integer, which is compatible with the data type counter of **Membership No (Membership)**. In one-to-many relationships the primary table in the relationship is the 'one' table, in this case the **Membership** table, and the related table is the 'many' table, i.e. the **Bookings** table. To define a relationship between tables:

5   Choose **Tools-Relationships** and the **Relationships** dialog box appears with the **Show Table** dialog box within it.

   If the **Show Table** dialog box does not appear click on the **Show Table** button on the toolbar.

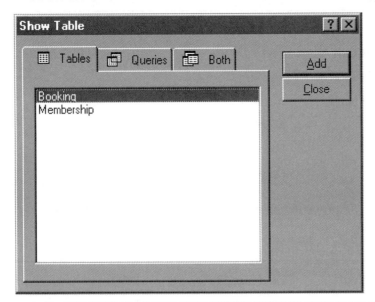

6   Select Membership and click on **Add** . Select Bookings and click on **Add** . Click on **Close** .
   The two table windows should be displayed. You may resize them if you wish.

7   To create the relationship click on the **Membership No** field in the **Membership** table and drag to the **Membership No** in the **Bookings** table.

This displays a Relationships dialog box.

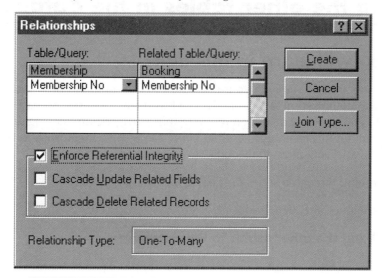

8   Click in the **Enforce Referential Integrity** check box then click on **Create**, and the relationship between the tables will be shown.

9   Use **File-Save** to save changes to the layout and close the **Relationships** dialog box.

Defining the other tables in the database

What you will learn in this unit

If you wish to use only one table in your database you may omit this unit. You will find that you can complete most of Units 10 to 31 as many exercises are based on the Membership table. You should then return to this activity before moving on to Unit 32. This unit revisits techniques used in Units 2 to 8 so you may wish to refer back to these as you work through this unit.

The aim of this unit, through a series of tasks, is to:

■ reinforce techniques already introduced.

Task 1: Defining the other tables in the database

Create the following tables.

1   Click on the New button in the Database window to open the table design window.

2   Define the field types as shown.

3   For each table set the primary key, shown in bold italics, before closing the table.

Membership Category

Field name	Data type	Description
Category No	Number	A one-digit identification number
Category Type	Text	Categories are Senior, Senior Club, Junior, Junior Club, Concessionary, Youth Club
Membership Fee	Currency	

4   Define **Category No** as the primary key. Save the table as ***Membership Category*** and close the table.

Classes

Field name	Data type	Description
Class No	AutoNumber	
Class Day	Number	
Class Time	Date/Time	
Class Tutor	Text	
Class Activity	Text	
Male/Female/Mixed	Text	

5   Define **Class No** as the primary key. Save the table as ***Classes*** and close the table. **Class Day** has been chosen to be numeric, with 1 representing Sunday through to 7 representing Saturday. The reason for this is so that the classes can be listed in day and time order.

In your database window you should see four tables listed.

Task 2: Defining field properties for the other tables

1   Open each table in turn, in Design view.

2   Amend the field properties as shown below.

3   Save and close the tables.

Membership Category table

Field	Property	Setting
Category No	Field Size	Byte
	Required	Yes
Category Type	Field Size	15
	Required	Yes
Membership Fee	Required	Yes

Classes table

Field	Property	Setting
Class Day	Field Size	Byte
	Required	Yes
Class Time	Format	Short time (equivalent to hh:mm)
	Required	Yes
Class Tutor	Field Size	30
Class Activity	Field Size	20
	Required	Yes
Male/Female/Mixed	Field Size	10
	Validation Rule	"Male" or "Female" or "Mixed"
	Validation Text	Please enter Male, Female or Mixed

Task 3: Creating indexes

In this task, indexes for the **Classes** and **Bookings** tables are created.

1 Open the **Classes** table in Design view.

2 Select the **Class Tutor** field and choose Yes (Duplicates OK) for the indexed property.

3 Repeat for **Class Activity**, choosing Yes (Duplicates OK) for the indexed property. Close and save changes.

4 Open the **Bookings** table in design view.

5 Select the **Room/Hall/Court** field and choose Yes (Duplicates OK).

6 Set a multiple field index (refer back to Unit 5) using the fields **Date** and **Time**. Close and save changes.

Task 4: Defining the other relationships

There are two other relationships in the database (see FIGURE 2.1). These are:

- between the **Classes** table and the **Bookings** table
- between the **Membership Category** table and the **Membership** table.

Both these relationships are one-to-many relationships. Using the **Relationships** dialog box, set these relationships up as follows:

1 Choose **Tools-Relationships**.

2   Add the tables **Classes** and **Membership Category** using the Show Table dialog box. Display this dialog box by clicking on the `Show Table` button on the toolbar.

3   To create the relationship click on the **Class No** field in the Classes table and drag to the **Class No** in the **Bookings** table.

Note that the direction of dragging is one to many.

4   Click in the Enforce Referential Integrity check box then click on `Create`, and the relationship between the tables will be shown.

5   If you try to create the relationship between **Category No** in the **Membership Category** table and **Category No** in the **Membership** table you will find that if you check the Enforce Referential Integrity check box, Access will not create the relationship because there is no data in the **Membership Category** table. When the data is added in Unit 17 the relationship can be created. Close the Relationships dialog box.

Task 5: Documenting the table definitions

 Use **Tools-Analyze Documentor** to print the documentation for these two newly created tables, in the same manner as for the **Membership** table (Unit 5).

Designing a basic query

What you will learn in this unit

This unit introduces the ability of databases to answer questions asked of them. The information stored in a database is of no use unless it can be retrieved, and then only if it can be retrieved in a way so as to be useful. Data stored in a telephone directory can be retrieved, for example, by knowing the name and address of someone in the directory and using the database to find the telephone number.

By the end of this unit you should be able to:

- question the database by creating a query

- view the result of the query

- save a query so that it can be retrieved for later use

- print out your query.

There are many reasons for using queries. They have a very important role in database systems. Queries are used:

- so that online search and retrieval of specfic records can be made. For example, to look at a particular set of members for editing, or to view the bookings for a given room on a certain day, or to find the class tutors who have a particular qualification.

- for creating forms and printing reports. Queries retrieve a particular set of records and fields; reports are used to print this information. A form based on a query can be used to restrict data entry to certain fields. Units 14 to 20 introduce forms and reports.

Queries may be based on more than one table, but in this session all of the queries will be based on the **Membership** table. You will see later in Unit 32 how to create queries based on more than one table.

The Simple Query Wizard and query design window

Creating a query involves two aspects:

- selecting the fields that are to be shown in the query. It is not usually necessary to retrieve all fields; for example, the name and the telephone number of a member may be all that is needed for a telephone survey of a particular group of members.

- selecting the records that are to be shown in the query. For this, Access provides a method of querying by which you can describe the characteristics of the data that you are looking for. This method is know as Query by Example (QBE) and is achieved by allowing you to give examples of the data that you are searching for in the form of criteria.

Simple Query Wizard

The Simple Query Wizard helps you to design a simple select query. A select query will select fields from a table. The Wizard will ask you to select the table you wish to query and which fields you want in your query. It will create the query, which you can then modify later using the Query Design window.

Query Design window

The Query Design Window (FIGURE 10.1) allows a query to be designed that will select the required fields and records that you ask for. This window is in two sections: the upper section is where the table windows of the tables used in the query are displayed. In the lower section there is a grid for the query design. The two most important rows in the grid are Field and Criteria. Each column needs a field name; all of the fields in the table may be chosen or only a few of them. In the Criteria row an example of the data may be given. As you work your way through this session you will be introduced to the functions of the other rows in the grid.

FIGURE 10.1

Before asking questions of a database you must first decide which tables in the database are required to answer them. The following activities will describe how to ask questions of just one table, the **Membership** table. You will see later, in Unit 32, how to include more than one table in a query.

Displaying the Query Design window

■ Click on the **Query** tab in the Database window and click on the **New** button to create a new query.

■ If you have not created any queries yet then the **Open** and **Design** buttons are not available.

■ Select Design View in the New Query dialog box and click on **OK**. The Show Table dialog box appears in front of the Query Design window. This dialog box allows you to select all of the tables needed for the query.

■ Select a table and choose **Add** to add it to the query. When the selection of table(s) is complete click on the **Close** button.

Using the Simple Query Wizard to add fields to a query

After choosing Simple Query Wizard from the New Query dialog box, the Simple Query Wizard dialog box will be displayed (FIGURE 10.2).

FIGURE 10.2

From the **Table/Queries** drop-down list box select the table that the query is to be based on.

If you wish to add all of the fields to the query click on the ▧ **>>** button. If you want to add a selected set of fields, highlight each field and click on the ▧ **>** button. You may change your mind and use the ▧ **<<** button to remove all fields (so that you may start again) or use the ▧ **<** button to remove a selected field.

When the required fields have been chosen click on ▧ **Next >**. Select a Detail query and click on ▧ **Next >**. Give the query a title and click on ▧ **Finish**. The result of your query will be shown in Datasheet view.

Task 1: Selecting fields for a query using Simple Query Wizard

1 From the Database window click on the Query tab and click on the ▧ **New** button. Choose the Simple Query Wizard from the **New Query** dialog box.

2 From the **Table/Queries** drop-down list box in the **Simple Query Wizard** dialog box select the **Membership** table.

3 Add the fields **Membership No**, **Lastname**, **Sex** and **Date of Joining** to the query by highlighting each field in turn and clicking on the ▧ **>** button.

4 Click on ▧ **Next >**. Select a Detail query and click on ▧ **Next >**. Give the query the title *Dates of Joining* and click on ▧ **Finish**.
The result of your query will be shown in Datasheet view.

5 View and close the query window.
The name of the query is listed in the Database window.

Adding fields to a query without using the Wizard

By choosing Design view from the **New Query** dialog box, the **Show Table** box will be displayed in front of the Query Design window. After choosing the table for the query, it will be displayed in the upper section of the query design window, as shown in FIGURE 10.1. The next step is to decide which fields in that table you wish to include in the query. Later we will explore query criteria that allow us to select specific records. The query is designed in the lower section of the Query Design window.

Adding all the fields in the table to the query

The simplest case is where we want to include all of the fields in the table:

1 Double-click on the title bar of the field list box of the table in the upper section of the window. This selects all of the fields.

2 Click on any of the selected fields (not the *) and drag to the Field cell in the lower section of the Query window. The pointer should look like a set of record cards.

3 When you release the mouse button all of the field names will have been added to the query. Use the horizontal scroll bar to move to the right because all of the columns will not fit on the screen.

Adding individual fields in the table to the query

There are three ways of adding the fields one by one to a query. The first method is by double-clicking, thus:

1 Double-click on the name of the field required in the field list box in the upper section of the window. It will appear in the next available column in the grid below.

The second is to use the drop-down list associated with each field cell, thus:

1 Click in the Field cell in the lower section of the window. A **List Box** button appears at the end of the cell.

2 Click on the **List Box** button and a drop-down list of field names will appear.

3 Select the name of the field required (if necessary, scroll through the list), click on it and it will appear in the Field cell (FIGURE 10.3).

FIGURE 10.3

The third way is to use the drag-and-drop method, thus:

1 Click on the name of the field required in the field list box in the upper section of the window.

2 Drag and drop this field into the required field cell in the lower part of the Query window. While doing this the pointer should look like one record card.

3 If you drop the field onto a column containing a field, then a column will be inserted to contain the new field.

Removing fields from the query

Fields may be removed singly or in blocks from the query. To remove all of the fields from the query:

1 Select the first column by clicking on the bar at the top of the column (the pointer will change shape to a down arrow); drag to select all of the columns.

2 Press the *Delete key* or choose **Edit-Delete**.

To remove an individual field from the query, just select the required column for deleting and use **Edit-Delete**.

Viewing or running a query

To see the result of a query, either click on the Datasheet button or the Run Query button in the toolbar. To return to the query design click on the Design button next to the Datasheet button on the toolbar.

Design button   Datasheet button   Run Query button

Access displays a datasheet containing the records that match the query with fields as defined in the query. This query result is what Access calls a dynaset. A dynaset is a temporary table and is not a permanent part of your database. If you modify your query the resulting dynaset will change accordingly.

Task 2: Selecting fields for a query

In this task the Membership table will be queried; data from all records will be shown in the dynasets. Initially all fields will be shown and then you will see how to select only certain fields.

1 Starting from the Database window, click on the Queries tab.

2 Click on New to open a new query.

3 Select the table **Membership** from the **Add Table** dialog box and close the dialog box.

4 Add all of the fields to the query, following the first method described above.

5 Click on the Datasheet button on the toolbar.
  You should see the whole of the table forming the dynaset.

6 Click on the Design button on the toolbar to return to the Query Design window.

7 Remove all of the fields from the query, following the method described above.

8 Add fields individually to the query, experimenting with the different methods described above. Add the fields **Membership No**, **Lastname**, **Sex** and **Date of Joining**.

9 Click on the **Datasheet** or **Run Query** button on the toolbar.

You should see only these fields from all of the records of the table forming the dynaset.

10 Click on the **Design** button on the toolbar to return to the Query Design window.

11 By adding and removing fields, alter the fields in your query so that they are **Lastname**, **Sex**, **Category No** and **Sporting Interests**.

12 Click on the **Datasheet** button on the toolbar, or the **Run Query** button.

You should see only these fields from all of the records of the table forming the dynaset.

Saving a query

Sometimes you may wish to ask the same question of a database over and over again; for example, is a membership subscription due? As time passes members need to renew their membership and it is useful to be able to send reminders. A query designed to do this would be saved so that it could be used repeatedly. To save a query:

■ Choose File-Save

■ In the **Query Name** box of the **Save As** dialog box enter a name that will remind you what the query is about. The name can be up to 255 characters. Click on **OK**.

■ If you close the Query window, you will see the name of your query in the Queries list of the Database window, from where it can be opened for use on another occasion.

Closing and opening a query

To close a query, either:

■ Double-click on the query's control menu button, or

■ Choose **File-Close**.

You can open an existing query in either Design view or Datasheet view.

To open a query in Design view:

■ In the Database window, click on the **Query** button.

■ Select the query you want to open, and then click on the **Design** button.

To open a query in Datasheet view:

■ In the Database window, click on the **Query** button.

■ Select the query you want to open, and then click on the **Open** button.

Task 3: Saving a query

In this task the query created at the end of the previous task will be saved.

1   Choose **File-Save**.

2   Give the name ***Members Sporting Interests*** to this query and click on **OK**.

3   Close the query. You should see the name of the query in the Database window.

Printing a query

Before printing the dynaset produced by your query it is advisable to preview it first. To preview a query table:

■ In the datasheet view, click on the **Print Preview** button on the toolbar. You will be shown a preview which displays a miniature version of what is to be printed.

■ The pointer becomes a magnifying glass and can be use to zoom-in to the page. If you use other Windows applications you will be familiar with this. Clicking will toggle between zoom-in and zoom-out modes. When zoomed-in, the vertical and horizontal scroll bars can be used to scroll around your previewed page.

■ To adjust the column widths you need to return to the Datasheet view. To do this close the preview window. The column widths are adjusted in the same way as for table datasheets, as described in Unit 7.

Once you are satisfied that the preview is correct, then, from the Print Preview mode:

■ Choose **File-Print**. The **Print** dialog box appears. If you want to print without changing anything then *skip the following three steps*. Note: to print directly without displaying the **Print** dialog box, click on the **Print** button on the toolbar.

■ Click on the **Setup** button and the **Page Setup** dialog box will appear.

■ To change the margins click in the appropriate box and edit the default setting You can select the orientation of the page, the printer and the paper size. The **Print Headings** check box, if not checked, will suppress the printing of the field names as headings. Click on **OK** to return to the **Print** dialog box.

■ Click on **OK**. Click on the **Close** button to return to the query datasheet.

Task 4: Printing

In this task the dynaset produced by the query created in Task 3 will be printed.

1   From the Database window open the query in Datasheet view.

2   Click on the **Print Preview** button on the toolbar.

3 Some columns may need widening. [Close] the preview window to return to the datasheet and widen the columns (see *Customising the datasheet layout*, Unit 7).

4 Preview again. Zoom in to check that the columns are wide enough, and click on the [Print] button.

5 Click on [OK] in the **Print** dialog box and the following dynaset should be printed:

Surname	Sex	Category No	Sporting Interests
Walker	Yes	2	Tennis, squash
Cartwright	No	1	Aerobics, swimming, running, squash
Perry	Yes	6	Judo, Karate
Forsythe	No	2	
Jameson	No	1	Aerobics, squash
Robinson	No	3	Swimming, Judo
Harris	Yes	5	Badminton, cricket
Shangali	Yes	2	Weight training
Barrett	No	1	Keep fit, swimming
Weiner	Yes	1	Weight training, squash
Ali	Yes	6	Judo, swimming, football
Young	No	2	Keep fit, Aerobics, squash
Gray	Yes	5	
Swift	No	5	
Davies	No	1	Aerobics, squash, swimming
Robinson	No	1	Tennis, Aerobics
Everett	Yes	2	Squash, Fitness training, football
Locker	Yes	4	
Locker	No	4	
Jones	Yes	1	Weight training

6 Click on the [Close] button to return to the datasheet view.

Deleting a query

Some queries may only be used once, in which case it is not really worth saving them. Queries that will be used more than once should be saved, but a query may have a limited usefulness or be superseded by another query. Therefore, from time to time, some queries will need to be removed.

Take care when removing a query. Later, we will see that reports and forms can be based upon queries, so it is important to assign these to alternative queries or to delete them as well. At present there is nothing based on the queries we have created and they may be safely deleted.

To delete a query, in the Database window click on the **Queries** tab to display the queries. Highlight the query that is to be deleted and press *Delete*.

Task 5: Deleting a query

In this task the query created using the Simple Query Wizard will be deleted.

1   Display the queries in the Database window.

2   Select the query created by the Wizard, **Dates of Joining**, and press *Delete*

3   Reply Yes to confirm the delete operation.

Sorting the dynaset

What you will learn in this unit

The dynaset or result of a query can be displayed in different orders. If no sorting order is specified then the records in the datasheet will be shown in their natural order, i.e. the order in which they were entered into the table. Sorting is particularly useful; for example, if the records are shown in order of date of birth then it is easier to see an age profile; if records are shown in order of town then geographical information becomes apparent. If a report is to be created from the query (see Unit 19) then the order of the records can be defined by the query.

By the end of this unit you should be able to:

■ sort the information shown in the answer to your query.

Sorting the dynaset

You may wish to see your result in a particular order, for example, in alphabetical order of surnames or according to postal area, etc. In the grid in the lower section of the Query Design window there is a sort row. To define the type of sorting:

1 Click in the sort cell for the field in which you are interested. A list box button appears at the end of the cell.

2 Clicking on the list box button will reveal the sorting choices: ascending, descending or not sorted. Ascending will sort from low to high, descending from high to low and not sorted will not apply any sorting.

 There is an order of priority of sorting when more than one field is being sorted. The order of priority is determined by the order of the fields in the query, leftmost fields being of higher priority.

Task 1: Sorting

This task investigates the different orders in which the **Members Sporting Interests** query created in Task 3 of Unit 10 can be displayed.

1   From the Design view of this query, click in the sort cell for the **Lastname** field.

2   Open the list box and choose Ascending.

3   Display the dynaset, by clicking on the **Run Query** button. Return to the Design view.

4   Change the sort order of the **Lastname** field to (not sorted).

5   Choose Ascending as the order for the **Sex** field.

6   Display the dynaset. Return to the Design view.

7   Choose Ascending order for the Lastname and Descending order for the Sex fields. In what order do you expect the data for the twins to be shown? View the dynaset.

8   Close the query without saving it.

Task 2: Sort order priority

For this task a simple query will be created to illustrate the effect that the order of the fields in the query has upon the priority of sort order. By choosing different priorities and viewing the resulting dynaset, the effect can be appreciated.

1   Create a new query using the **Membership** table.

2   Add the fields **Category No**, **Town** and **Lastname** to this query.

3   Choose Ascending as the order for both the **Category No** and **Town** fields.

4   Run the query to view the resulting dynaset.

5 Return to the Query Design window and select the **Category No** field by clicking at the top of the column (while the pointer looks like a down-pointing arrow). With the column selected point to the field header at the top of the column (the pointer should be left-pointing arrow shape); click and drag to reposition it after the **Town** field. Leave the sort order of **Category No** as ascending.

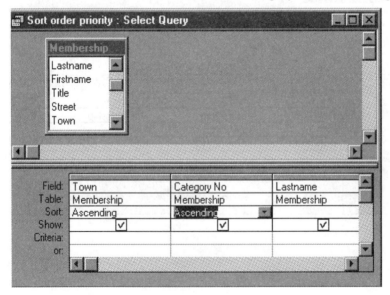

6   View the resulting dynaset, which should be in a different order from the
    previous one.

7   Close this query without saving it.

Using query criteria

What you will learn in this unit

There are many reasons for asking questions. In business, questions are important in decision making. A database management system can make for very effective questioning of data relating to, for example, marketing or management. In the case of Chelmer Leisure and Recreation Centre, the answers to the questions above can help with decisions regarding:

- whether the centre attracts mainly local members; the effect of local competition
- no-smoking areas being introduced
- the introduction of activities and facilities for the older members
- the introduction of discount scheme for loyal members
- fees charged for various categories.

To ask questions, criteria need to be set, and these criteria are entered into the criteria cells of the Query Design grid. Querying is done by example, so an example of the answer to the question is entered into the criteria cell.

By the end of this unit you should be able to:

- enter query criteria
- rename and hide fields in a query
- use logic in queries.

Entering query criteria

Query criteria basically allow the enquirer to frame questions that enable specific records to be retrieved from the database. We might want to find out various things using the data stored in a table. For example, some questions that might be asked about the **Membership** table are:

- Which members live in Chelmer?
- Which members smoke?
- Which members are over 60?
- Which members joined before 1/1/92?
- Which members are in categories 1 and 2?

Task 1: Query criteria for the membership table

In this task the questions listed above will be formulated as queries for the **Membership** table. The queries use the datatypes Text, Number, Date and Yes/No. Each question will be dealt with in turn.

1 Create a new query using the **Membership** table.

2 Add all of the fields to the query.

Which members live in Chelmer?

1 In the **Criteria** cell of the **Town** field type *Chelmer*.	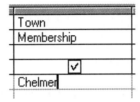

2 Click on the **Datasheet** or **Run Query** button.	The resulting dynaset should only contain records for which the **Town** field is equal to Chelmer.
3 Return to the Design view.	Notice that Access puts double quotation marks around your criterion if it thinks it is text.
4 Delete the criterion "Chelmer". Select the cell by double-clicking and press *Delete* to clear the cell.	Alternatively, click in the cell and use the backspace key to delete the criterion.

Which members smoke?

1 In the **Criteria** cell of the **Smoker** field type *Yes*.	You may need to scroll to the right to display this cell on the screen.

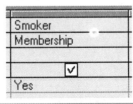

2 Click on the **Datasheet** or **Run Query** button and view the resulting dynaset.	
3 Return to the Design view. Delete the last criterion.	

Which members are over 60?

1 In the **Criteria** cell of the
 Date of Birth field type *<1/1/36*.

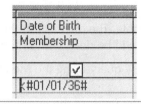

2 Click on the **Datasheet** or
 Run Query button and view
 the resulting dynaset. Return to
 the Design view.

Notice that Access has recognised your
query example as a date and converted
it to *<#01/01/36#*.

3 Delete this criterion.

Which members joined before 1/1/92?

1 In the Criteria cell of the Date of
 Joining field type *<1/1/92*.

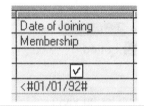

2 Click on the **Datasheet** or
 Run Query button and view
 the resulting dynaset.

3 Return to the Design view.
 Delete this criterion.

Which members are in categories 1 and 2?

1 In the **Criteria** cell of the **Category**
 No field type *<=2*.

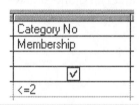

2 Click on the **Datasheet** or
 Run Query button and view
 the resulting dynaset.

3 Return to the Design view.
 Delete this criterion.

4 Close the query without saving it.

Renaming and hiding fields in a query

When queries are printed it is sometimes necessary to widen the column so that the field name at the top of the column can be seen. This in turn can lead to unnecessarily wide columns, so it is useful to be able to rename the field. The field header can be renamed in a query with an alternative name. For example, Last Renewed instead of Date of Last Renewal.

 Renaming the field header does not affect the name of the field in the underlying table.

To change field header names:

1 Switch to Query Design mode by clicking on the Query Design button. Move the insertion point to the column containing the field header name you wish to change.

2 Point to the beginning of the field header and click. The aim is to put the flashing insertion point at the beginning of the header name. If you accidentally select the header press *F2* to de-select it. If the insertion point is not at the beginning, then press the *Home* key to move it to the first character position.

3 Type in the new name for the field, and follow the name with a colon (FIGURE 12.1). Do not put a space between the name and the colon. The colon separates the name you type from the existing field name, which moves to the right to make room for your addition.

4 Click on the Datasheet button or the Run Query button and the query result with amended field header will be displayed.

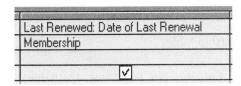

FIGURE 12.1

In the previous two units you have seen how to select the fields you want to see in the result of a query and how to impose criteria. These can be combined so that the dynaset is only the records that match the criteria and contains only the fields specified in the query. To be able to impose a criterion on a field, that field needs to be in the query grid, which means that it will form part of the dynaset. This may not always be desirable, so Access offers the choice of whether or not the field forms part of the dynaset. By default, all fields in the query show in the dynaset as the 'Show' cell is on; to hide a field click in the box in the Show cell. The tick disappears and the field will not form part of the dynaset.

Task 2: Renaming and hiding fields in a query

Query 1: This query lists the names and addresses of all the male members who are smokers.

1   Create a new query using the **Membership** table.

2   Add the following fields: **Membership No, Title, Lastname, Street, Town, County, Post Code, Smoker, Sex.**

3   In the criteria fields of **Smoker** and **Sex** put *Yes*. Hide these fields.

4   Sort the **Lastname** field in ascending order.

5   Rename **Membership No** as **Member No** and display the dynaset.

Member No	Title	Lastname	Street	Town	County	Post Code
13	Mr	Gray	4 The Parade	Chelmer	Cheshire	CH1 7ER
7	Mr	Harris	55 Coven Road	Chelmer	Cheshire	CH3 8PS
20	Mr	Jones	17 Mayfield Av.	Chelmer	Cheshire	CH2 9OL
1	Mr	Walker	16 Dovecot Cl.	Chelmer	Cheshire	CH2 6TR

6   Save the query as ***Addresses of Male Smokers***. Close the query.

Query 2: This query looks at the occupations of the female members of the centre. The result of this query will be selected fields from selected records.

1   Create a new query using the **Membership** table.

2   Add the following fields to the query: **Category No, Firstname, Lastname, Occupation, Sex.**

3   In the criteria cell of the **Sex** field type *No*.

4   Click on the check box in the **Show** cell of the **Sex** field to hide it.

5   Click at the beginning of the **Category No** header and type *Cat:*
    Do not type a space before the colon.

6   Click on the **Datasheet** or **Run Query** button to view the result of the query. The **Category No** field should have the header Cat and the **Sex** field should be hidden.

7   Save the query as ***Occupations of Female Members***.

Exploring types of query criteria

The queries that have been created so far in this session have only used criteria in one field. Criteria may be applied to all of the fields that are included in a query. Each field may be sorted or hidden. By combining these, more complex queries can be produced.

We have already used some of the operators used in criteria. The following table summarises them:

Operator	Meaning
Mathematical operators	
<	less than
>	greater than
<>	not equal to
>=	greater than or equal to
<=	less than or equal to
+	addition
-	subtraction
*	multiplication
/	division
Text operators	
"J*"	text strings beginning with J
"*ton"	text strings ending with ton
"*k*"	text strings containing the letter k

Using logic in queries

Queries can be asked that use queries on more than one field, for example, male smokers (Query 1 in Task 2). The question is: 'Is the member male AND does he smoke?'. There is a logical AND between the two criteria: both criteria must be true for the record to be retrieved.

What if a logical AND is required on the same field; for example, members whose date of joining was after 1/1/92 AND before 1/1/93 (Query 2 in Task 3)? In the criteria cell the word 'and' is used between the two criteria, for example, **>=1/1/92 and <1/1/93**. More than two criteria may be specified but remember to put the word 'and' between them.

The other form of logic that is used in queries is OR. There is a row entitled **or:** in the Query Design grid. An example of this would be a query which requires as its answer the names and addresses of members who live in Chelmer OR Meirton. The way in which this query is set up is to enter ***Chelmer*** into the **criteria** row of the

73

Town field and underneath in the **or:** row to enter **Meirton**. The example query below (Query 3 in Task 3) lists the names of the members who are likely to use the fitness suite because their sporting interests are aerobics, fitness training or weight training.

Task 3: Using different types of query criteria

Query 1: Querying text fields. This query picks out people with particular sporting interests.

1 Create a new query using the **Membership** table.

2 Add the following fields: **Membership No**, **Lastname**, **Category No**, **Sporting Interests**.

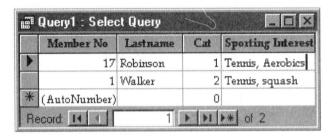

Member No	Lastname	Cat	Sporting Interest
17	Robinson	1	Tennis, Aerobics
1	Walker	2	Tennis, squash
(AutoNumber)		0	

Record: 1 of 2

3 In the **criteria** fields of **Sporting Interests** type **"*Tennis*"**.
   Access will convert this to read **Like "*Tennis*"**.

4 Sort the **Lastname** field in ascending order.

5 Rename **Membership No** as **Member No** and **Category No** as **Cat**.

6 Display the dynaset.

7 Print the dynaset.

8 Save the query, giving it the name **Sporting Interest**, and close the query.

Query 2: Logic, using AND. This query picks out members who joined in 1992.

1 Create a new query using the **Membership** table.

2 Add the following fields: **Title, Firstname, Lastname, Telephone No, Date of Joining**.

3 In the **criteria** field of **Date of Joining** type *>=1/1/92 and <1/1/93*.
   Access will convert this to read *>=#01/01/92# And <#01/01/93#*.

4 Hide the **Date of Joining** field.

5 Sort the **Lastname** field in ascending order.

6 Display the dynaset.

7 Print the dynaset.

8 Save the query, giving it the name ***When joined***, and close the query.

Query 3: Logic using OR. This query picks out members whose sporting interests are either aerobics, fitness training or weight training and shows their home town so that local interest can be assessed.

1 Create a new query using the **Membership** table.

2 Add the following fields: **Membership No, Category No, Lastname, Town, Sporting Interests**

3   In the criteria field of **Sporting Interests** type "*aerobics*".
    Access will convert this to read *Like "*aerobics*"*.

4   In the **or:** field of **Sporting Interests** type *"*fitness training*"*.

5   In the row below type *"*weight training*"*.

6   Hide the **Sporting Interests** field.

7   Sort the **Lastname** field in ascending order.

8   Display the dynaset.
    Notice that when querying text Access is not case sensitive: *"*aerobics*"* will
    find *aerobics*, *AEROBICS* or *Aerobics*.

9   Print the dynaset.

10 Close the query without saving.

More complex queries

What you will learn in this unit

At the end of this unit you will be able to:

- edit and rename a query
- create new fields by calculation
- count and average fields, and group and average fields
- use criteria in a summary query.

Queries can perform calculations on the data in the table. Calculations may be to count the number of records, to add up or take the average of certain fields or to create new fields by calculation. In Task 1 a new field, 'Age', is created and the average age of the members is calculated. A new field can be created from a calculation using existing fields in the table. For example, if there is a price field that does not include sales tax then a Sales Tax field can be calculated by multiplying the price by the rate of the tax.

There are a wide range of different applications where it might be appropriate to perform calculations as part of a query. Here we briefly explain some of the basic concepts and give a few examples.

To create a calculated field, in the next empty field cell enter an expression to calculate the new field. The expression takes the form **Name of calculated field:Expression**. The expression is the formula for creating the value of this field. An expression involves other fields and these are written enclosed in square brackets; for example, **Taxable pay:[Gross Pay]-[Free Pay] or VAT:[Cost]*0.175**.

Expressions may be used with date data types and there are several date functions available. The two that are used in Task 1 are:

- Year(), which returns the year of the date/time value enclosed in brackets as an integer number; for example Year([Date of Joining]) might result in 1992
- Now(), which returns the date and time of the computer's system clock.

Sometimes it is useful to produce some summary statistics as a result of your query, for example the number of fields, the total of values in those fields or the average of the fields. These statistics may be for all the records in the table or just for the ones

selected by the query. Click on the **Totals** or **'Sigma'** button on the toolbar

to gain access to the statistics functions, which can be entered into the **Total** row which appears when the Totals button is depressed (FIGURE 13.1).

FIGURE 13.1

Each cell in the **Total:** row has its own drop-down list. Various statistical functions are available:

Function	Purpose
Count	gives the number of records
Sum	gives a total of all values in that particular field
Min, Max	gives the maximum or minimum value of that particular field
Avg, StDev, Var	the average, standard deviation, and variance of a particular field
Group by	groups records according to this field, producing summary statistics for each group
Where	allows criteria to be specified

Editing and renaming a query

Once a query has been saved it can be used again and again. More records may be added to the table; each time a query is used it uses the data currently held in the table. However, as a database develops then a query may be changed to accommodate changing requirements. If the query is modified it may be advisable to change its name so that it remains as meaningful as possible.

Task 1: Creating a new field by calculation

1   Create a new query using the **Membership** table.

2   Add the fields **Category No** and **Lastname**.

3   Click in the next field cell and create a calculated field by typing
    Age:Year(Now())-Year([Date of Birth]).

4   Sort the **Age** field in descending order.

Age: Year(Now())-Year([Date of Birth])
Descending
☑

5   Display the dynaset.

6   Print the dynaset.

7   Save the query with the name ***Member ages***.

Task 2: Counting and averaging fields

Continue with the query created in Task 1.

1   Click on the **Totals** button to display the **Total:** row.

2   In the Total cell for the first two fields select Count.

3   In the Total cell for the **Age** field type ***Avg***.

Field:	Lastname	Category No	Age: Year(Now())-Year([Date of Birth])
Table:	Membership	Membership	
Total:	Count	Count	Avg
Sort:			Descending
Show:	☑	☑	☑
Criteria:			
or:			

4   Run the query.

The result of this query is different from the normal dynaset display. One row is displayed which contains summary information according to the specification in the Total row. Returning to the Design view and clicking on the **Totals** button will cause the Total row to disappear, and the query reverts to that in Task 1.

CountOfCategory	CountOfSurname	Age
20	20	32

If you save the summary form of this query, and close it, when you open it again, notice that Access will have changed the calculated field to ***Age: Avg(Year(Now())-Year([Date of Birth]))*** and put ***Expression*** in the Total row.

Task 3: Grouping and averaging fields

Continue with the query in Task 2, by returning to the Query Design window.

1   In the Total cell for the **Category No** field select Group by and choose Ascending
as the sort order for this field.

2   Remove the sort order from **Age** and arrange your query as illustrated below:

Field:	Category No	Lastname	Age: Avg(Year(Now())-Year([Date of Birth]))
Table:	Membership	Membership	
Total:	Group By	Count	Expression
Sort:	Ascending		
Show:	✓	✓	✓
Criteria:			
or:			

3   Run the query.

This time a row for each category is displayed containing in the **Age** field the
average age of members in each membership category.

Category No	CountOfSurname	Age
1	7	31.28571428571
2	5	36.4
3	1	10
4	2	11
5	3	60
6	2	13.5

Task 4: Using criteria in a summary query

Continue with the previous query by returning to the Query Design window.

1   In the Total cell for the **Category No** field select Where.

2   In the Criteria row put *1 or 2* (this is equivalent to putting *1* in the **Criteria** row
and *2* in the Or row).

3   Remove the sort order from **Category No**.

4 Hide the **Category No** field.

Field:	Lastname	Age: Avg(Year(Now())-Year([Date of Birth]))	Category No
Table:	Membership		Membership
Total:	Count	Expression	Where
Sort:			
Show:	✓	✓	☐
Criteria:			1 Or 2
or:			

5 Run the query.

The result should be the total number of members in categories 1 and 2 and their average age.

CountOfLastna	Age
12	33.41666666667

6 Try this for categories 3 and 4.

7 Save the query.

8 Rename this query as **Average Ages**.

9 With **Member Ages** selected in the database window, choose **Edit-Rename** and change the name to *Average Ages*.

Task 5: Additional queries

This task takes the form of a series of questions plus the rationale for the questions. All queries are created using the **Membership** table.

1 What are the occupations of women members whose sporting interests include aerobics?

If a large majority of women members whose sporting interests include aerobics have stated that they are housewives, then a ladies' aerobics class could be scheduled in the day rather than the evening. The fields that might be appropriate for this query, in addition to **Sporting Interests** and **Sex**, are **Membership No**, **Category No**, **Title**, **Firstname**, **Lastname** and **Occupation**. Try sorting on **Category No**.

2 What are the home towns of male members whose sporting interests include weight training?

Does the centre offer better weight training facilities than the local competition and so attract members from a wide area? The fields that might be appropriate for

81

this query, in addition to **Sporting Interests** and **Sex**, are **Firstname**, **Lastname**, **Category No** and **Town**. Sort on the **Town** field in ascending order.

3 Which members joined the centre between 1/1/93 AND 1/1/94?

This query can easily be created by referring to the second query in Task 3 in Unit 12. Such queries can be used to assess the success of the centre.

4 Which members are aged between 18 AND 25?

Should the bar consider holding social events targeted at this age group? Are there enough members locally in this age group to make this worthwhile? The fields that might be appropriate for this query are **Lastname**, **Firstname**, all address fields and **Sporting Interests**. Sort the query in Post Code order in Ascending order.

5 Which members are either housewives OR unemployed OR retired?

Technically this query ought to include househusbands, although there are none listed in the data given for members! The centre may consider a range of daytime activities which would appeal to this group of members. The fields that might be appropriate for this query are **Membership No**, **Category No**, **Date of Birth** and **Sex**. Sort the query in Date of Birth order.

6 Which members have sporting interests of keep fit AND aerobics?

The fields that might be appropriate for this query are **Membership No**, **Lastname**, **Category No** and **Date of Birth**. Sort in ascending order both the Category No and Date of Birth, with Category No having the higher priority.

Designing and using screen forms

What you will learn in this unit

In this unit you will learn how to create a screen form. A screen form provides a
more user-friendly way with which to work with your data. Entering data can be
made easier and less prone to error. At the end of the session you will be able to:

- create a form using the Form Wizard

- save a form

- use a form

- print a form.

In Units 2 to 9 the tables for the Chelmer Leisure and Recreation Centre were
defined. Data was entered into the **Membership** table but as yet data has not been
entered into the other tables. In this and the following two units the data will be
entered into these tables. The data could be entered into these tables as it was for
the Membership data, using the Datasheet view of the table. The disadvantage of
using the Datasheet view is that the fields in a record often do not all fit on the
screen. Also, viewing and entering data in the datasheet grid can be somewhat
tiresome.

When data is collected manually it is often by means of filling out a form. In a form
there are boxes to fill in with, for example, name, address etc, and there may be
boxes that are ticked, for example Yes/No boxes. Access offers the facility to create a
form on the screen so that data can be entered into a table by simply filling in the
form. Filling in such a form should be more user-friendly than filling in the cells in
a datasheet, provided that the form has been designed carefully.

A form can be based upon a table or a view created from a query. A query can use
more than one table so the form created from such a query can be used to enter data
into several different tables. This will be explored in later sessions. In this session we
will concentrate on designing forms to enter data into the tables in the database. It is
usual to have a form for each table of data for the purpose of entering and editing
data in that table.

Forms can be used to enter, edit, display and print data contained in your tables.
They offer the advantage of presenting data, on screen, in an organised and attractive
manner.

Standard forms are created for most applications or jobs, for example, a form for
entering the details of a new member, as shown in FIGURE 14.1.

Access allows you to create forms to your own design, for which it provides a wide
range of tools. If you are a new Access user, or simply for convenience, the Form

Wizard provides a quick and easy way to create a basic form. This basic form can be customised later. To enable us to get started quickly on form design we will make use of the Form Wizard.

FIGURE 14.1

Creating a form with AutoForm

There are three types of form that can be created using AutoForm: columnar, tabular and datasheet. A columnar form will display data from one record at a time. Tabular and datasheet forms are very similar in that they display more than one record at once. Because of the tabular format, if there are a lot of fields in the records then an entire record will not fit on the screen.

AutoForm will create a form instantly using all fields in the records of the underlying table that you choose to base your form upon. To create a form using AutoForm, starting from the Database window, either:

- click on the **From** tab and then click on the **New** button, or
- click on the **New Object** button in the toolbar, select New Form and a **New Form** dialog box appears (FIGURE 14.2).

FIGURE 14.2

Click on the list box button of the 'Choose the table or query where the object's data comes from' box, to produce a list of tables and queries, and select the table for which you wish to create a form.

Select one of the AutoForm options and click on **OK** .

Creating a single-column form using Form Wizard

A single-column form is one that allows the user to input one record at a time. The form shown in FIGURE 14.1 started as a single column form but has been modified slightly. A single-column form has boxes to fill in for the fields of information required for that record. These boxes are arranged in a column. To create a single-column form, perform the two steps as above, then select Form Wizard, and click on **OK** . Check that the correct table is listed in the Tables/Queries box (if it isn't, select the right one).

The next stage is to choose which fields are to be on the form. The fields that you can have in the form are shown in the Available Fields box.

These can be transferred to the Selected Fields box by means of selecting each field

in turn and clicking on the > button.

If you wish to add all the fields in the table to the form then click on the button

You may set the order in which the fields appear on the form by selecting them in the order you desire.

The [<] button will remove a highlighted field from a form and [<<] will remove all the fields from the form.

Once you have added the required fields to the form continue by clicking on the [Next>] button.

Choose whether a columnar, tabular or datasheet form is required. The layout of these was discussed above.

You are then asked what kind of look you want for your form and are given a choice of various styles. An example of the look is shown to the left of the dialog box. Click on each style in turn to see what it would look like. On the first occasion a form is created choose Standard; the style can be modified later. The next thing you are asked for is a title. Key in an appropriate title for your form into the text box. Now click on the [Finish] button to display the form with data in it.

Saving and closing a form

Save a form by choosing **File-Save** or clicking on the [Save] button. If this is a new form that you have not yet saved then Access will prompt you for a filename with a **File-Save As** dialog box. If you wish later to save this form with a different name then use **File-Save As** and fill in the appropriate details in the dialog box.

Remember that there is a distinction between the name and the title of a form. The title is displayed at the top of the form window. The name you give when saving the form is the form's filename, which you need to be able to recognise when you want to open the form for use again. These names appear in the Database window when the Form tab is selected.

A form can be closed by using **File-Close** or by using the [Close] button of the form window. If the form or the latest modification has not been saved you will be prompted to save. When a form is closed its name (the one you gave to it when saving) will be shown in the database window when the Form tab is selected.

To open a form from the Database window, click on the [Form] tab, select the name of the form required and click on the [Open] button.

Task 1: Creating a columnar membership form using AutoForm

In this task a single-column membership form will be created, which can later be modified to look like the form shown in FIGURE 14.1. The order in which the fields are selected for the form are important, as will become apparent when the form is used to enter data. To create this form:

1   From the Database window click on the Form tab and click on the [New] button.

2   Display the list of tables in the **New Form** dialog box and select **Membership** from the list of tables. Select AutoForm: columnar and click on [OK].

Access creates a form with a title and a list of field names in a column with a corresponding list of data for the first record in another column. Notice that there are some differences between this form and the one shown in FIGURE 14.1. Customising the form will be considered in Unit 15.

3   Choose **File-Save** and give the form the name Membership.

4   Close the form.

Creating a tabular form

A tabular form is one that displays more than one record on the screen. The field names form headers for columns and the records are shown below in a table. The number of records displayed will depend upon the size of the window and the number of records in the table. If there are a lot of fields in a record it is unlikely that you will be able to see the complete record on the screen, and you will need to scroll to the right to display more of the fields. This type of form is suited to records with only a few fields, such as those in the **Membership Category** table. The advantage of this form is that it displays more than one record at a time.

A tabular form may be created either using AutoForm or Form Wizard. The following task considers creating a tabular form using the Form Wizard.

Task 2: Creating the membership category form

No data has been entered into the **Membership Category** table; this task will create a form that can later be used for this purpose.

1   First close any open form.

2   From the Database window with the Form tab depressed click on **New** .

3   In the **New Form** dialog box select the **Membership Category** table.

4   Select Form Wizard and click on **OK** .

5   Add all of the fields to the form and click on the **Next>** button.

6   Choose a tabular form with a standard style.

7   Give it the title *Membership Category*.

8   Click on the **Finish** button to display the form.

The difference between this form and the single-column form is that the fields are arranged in columns. The top of the column is headed by the field name. There is no data in this form so there is only one blank record to display. When records have been added, as we shall see later, then more than one record is shown in the form.

9   Save the form as ***MEMBERSHIP CATEGORY***.

10 Close the form.

Using a form

To use a form, first display the available forms in the Database window by clicking on the **Form** tab in that window. Open the form either by selecting it and clicking on **Open** or by double-clicking on its name.

You can use the form to look at the data in the table (or query) upon which it is based. Whether it is a single-column or tabular form, use the record movement keys in the status bar or the **Edit-Go** To menu to move around the records in your form. Using the *Page Up* and *Page Down* keys with a single-column form will display the next/previous record, whereas with a tabular form they will either page up or down a screenful of records.

Using the form to enter a new record into the table

Forms should be designed with this purpose in mind because this is their primary function. Entering data is a labour intensive task and the design of the form is important because it may be used for long periods by a person entering data.

To enter a new record using a form:

1 Go to the end of your records using the **New Record** button on the status bar. If your form is single-column press the *Page Down* key and a blank form appears. If your form is tabular click in the first field of the blank record shown at the end of your records.

2 Enter data for another record by filling in the boxes for each field. When you have completed each text box (control) press *Enter* or *Tab* to move to the next one.

3 Check boxes are used for Yes/No fields; checked is Yes, not checked No.

Task 3: Using a form to enter data into a table

In this task we shall enter data into the **Categories of Membership** table, using the tabular form just created.

1   Open the **Membership Category** form.

2   Enter data as shown below.
    As you enter each record it is saved to the **Membership Category** table.

3   Close the form.

4   Now that there is data in the form use **Tools-Relationships** to create the link between the **Membership Category** and **Membership** tables. Drag **Category No** (Membership Category) to **Category No** on the Membership table. Check in the Enforce Referential Integrity check box. Refer back to Unit 8.

Printing a form

Forms are designed primarily for screen use, i.e. they are intended for data to be entered via the computer and they display the data on screen. However, Access offers the facility to print from a form. Before printing a form, always preview it first. A form can be previewed from either the run or design view mode.

Previewing

Previewing will display a miniature version of what is to be printed. This allows the layout to be assessed so that adjustments can be made before printing.

To preview a form:

1 Click on the **Print Preview** button on the toolbar [icon], and a miniature version of what is to be printed will be displayed.

2 To zoom in and zoom out simply click anywhere on the preview, or use the **Zoom** button. Clicking on the right mouse button will allow you to select the degree of magnification.

3 Choose **File-Page Setup** to make adjustments, such as the orientation (portrait or landscape), the choice of printer and the width of the margins. Click on **OK** when the required adjustments have been made.

Printing

When you are satisfied that the preview is correct, printing may be done from either the preview screen or the form screen. To print from the preview screen:

1 Choose **File-Print**.

2 Select whether all or certain pages of the form will be printed and the number of copies. Click on **OK**.

To print from the form screen follow the procedure above.

Task 4: Printing the membership category form

To print this form:

1 Open the **Membership Category** form.

2 Click on the **Print Preview** button.

3 Experiment with zooming in and zooming out.

4 Use **File-Page Setup** and/or **File-Print** to make adjustments before printing. If no adjustments are necessary then click on the **Print** button.

5 Close the form.

Customising forms

What you will learn in this unit

Forms are constructed from a collection of individual design elements, which are called *controls*. If you are familiar with Windows applications you will be familiar with dialog boxes and the controls that they contain. The controls that appear on the forms created so far are:

■ labels, so that you know what each part of the form is for, and

■ text boxes, for entering data.

There are other controls, which will be introduced in Unit 21.

By the end of this unit you will have seen how to:

■ display the customising tools (toolbox, palette, properties and field list)

■ move and size controls

■ align controls

■ add text to a form

■ add the date

■ add headers and footers to a printed form.

Customising a form

A form may be modified so that it is easier for inexperienced users to enter information into the database. To modify a form you need to display the form in design mode (see the following section). AutoForm and Form Wizard are good ways of creating a form quickly. However, the resulting form is rather standardised in terms of vertical spacing between controls, fonts and colours, so you are likely to wish to make modifications.

Components of a form in design view

Component	Description
Form Header	contains text such as the form's title, but field headers and graphics may be put into a header section.
Detail	contains the controls (field labels, text boxes and check boxes) that display data from your table for which the form has been designed.

Form Footer	similar in function to the Form Header and may contain information such as the date.
Right Margin	the position of the right margin is indicated by a vertical line on the right edge of the form; it can be moved by clicking and dragging it.
Bottom Margin	a horizontal line that indicates the bottom margin of the form; it also can be positioned by clicking and dragging.
Scroll Bars	vertical and horizontal scroll bars enable movement of the form within its window.

If you have used a Form Wizard to create the form, only the header band and the detail band contain controls. The header band contains information that will always appear at the top of the form, usually the title of the form. The detail band contains the controls for displaying the data.

Form design view

So far in this series of units a form has only been opened in 'form run' or data view. This is the mode in which forms are usually run, where they display and, more importantly, accept data. A form can also be shown in design view, which allows modifications to be made to its layout. In design view data cannot be entered into the form; only the layout and appearance of the form can be changed. A form has a different appearance in design view, as illustrated in FIGURE 15.1.

FIGURE 15.1

Instead of data appearing in the controls, the field names appear. Text or controls may be selected and moved to achieve the desired layout.

Label and text box controls

A field usually has two controls, a label control in which the field name appears and a text box control in which the data will appear when the form is run.

Extra windows

Other features of design mode are the availability of rulers and grid, and design aids in the form of other small windows, the Toolbox, Field List and Properties Sheet.

The Toolbox offers a selection of tools by which controls and text may be added to the form; the Field List shows a list of fields in the table that the form was based upon; and the Properties sheet is a list of properties. The list of properties will depend upon what part of the form is selected. You will become familiar with these as you progress through the tasks. To display the Toolbox click on the Toolbox button or use **View-Toolbox**. To display the Field List click on the **Field List** button or choose **View-Field List**. To display the Properties sheet click on the **Properties** button on the toolbar or choose **View-Properties**.

The buttons are (from left to right) the **Field List** button, the **Toolbox** button and the **Properties** button.

Colour selection

 Colour selection can be made using the drop-down buttons on the formatting toolbar. These will be considered in Unit 27.

Opening a form in design view

To open a form in design view, from the Database window, click on the Form tab, select the name of the form required and click on the **Design** button.

Once a form is open you may switch between the form run (data) view and the design view by clicking on the button on the toolbar.

Form view   Design view

Moving and sizing controls

Before you can move or size a control you must select it. A control is selected by clicking anywhere on its surface. When selected the control is enclosed by an outlining rectangle with an anchor rectangle at its upper left corner and five smaller rectangles. These smaller rectangles are sizing handles. On columnar forms text boxes often have associated labels, and when you select one of these objects they are both selected together as a unit.

To...	Do this
Select a text box control and its label (if it has a label)	Click anywhere on either the label or the text box.
Move a text box control and its label (if it has a label)	After selecting, move the pointer over the label until it changes shape to a hand. Click and drag the label and entry box to the new position.
Move label or text box control separately	After selecting, move the pointer over the anchor handle at the top left corner of either the label or text box control. The pointer should change shape to a pointing hand. Click and drag to the new position.
Adjust the width and height of a control simultaneously	Move the pointer over one of the small sizing handles at one of the three corners. It should change to a diagonal two-headed arrow. Click and drag to size required.
Adjust only the height of the control	Move the pointer over one of the sizing handles on the horizontal surface of the outline. It should change shape to a vertical two-headed arrow. Click and drag to the height required.
Adjust only the width of the control	Move the pointer over one of the sizing handles on the vertical surface of the outline. It should change shape to a horizontal two-headed arrow. Click and drag to the width required.

Selecting and moving a group of controls

You can select and move more than one object at a time. This is useful if you want to keep the relative spacing of a group of objects yet want to move them to another part of the form.

To select a group of objects, do one of the following.

- Imagine that the group of objects is enclosed by a rectangle. Use the pointer and, by clicking and dragging, draw this rectangle on the form. When you release the mouse button, all of the objects within this rectangle will be selected.

- Select one object, hold down the *Shift* key while selecting the next and subsequent objects (this is easier when controls are in close proximity).

To move:

- the whole group: with the pointer as the shape of a hand, drag;

- an individual control in the group: point to its anchor handle and drag.

To deselect:

- one object in the group: click on it while holding down the *Shift* key;

- the whole group: click anywhere outside the selected area.

To move the group of objects click and drag the anchor handle of any of the objects in the group.

Using the ruler and the grid

The **View-Ruler** command will select whether or not the ruler is displayed. When a control is being dragged, indicator lines slide along both rulers to aid positioning of controls.

View-Grid will display or hide a grid of small dots, which are also an aid to the positioning of controls. The spacing of the grid can be adjusted by adjusting the setting of the GridX and GridY properties on the form's property sheet. To display the form property sheet use **Edit-Select Form** and click on the **Properties** button.

When **Format-Snap to Grid** is on, which is indicated by a tick next to **Snap to Grid** in the menu, any new controls drawn on the form will have their corners aligned to points on the grid. When Snap to Grid is off the control can be placed anywhere.

Aligning a group of controls

Once you start to move controls around the form they can become untidy as they become misaligned. By selecting a group of controls together, they can be aligned. Select labels and text boxes separately for alignment purposes. To align labels:

1 Select the labels by drawing a rectangle which encloses part or all of the labels you wish to select, as illustrated in FIGURE 15.2. Alternatively, click each label while holding down the *Shift* key.

2 Choose **Format-Align** and, as these are labels, select **Right**. The selected group of controls should all align to the right.

FIGURE 15.2

To align text box controls:

1 Select the text box controls by drawing a rectangle which encloses part or all of the text boxes you wish to select, or click each text box while holding down the *Shift* key (FIGURE 15.3).

2 Choose **Format-Align** and, as these are text boxes, select **Left**. The selected group of controls should all align to the left.

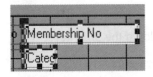

FIGURE 15.3

Changing the form's area

The area of each section of a form, the header, detail and footer sections, may be altered individually. Also, the position of the right and bottom edges of a form may be adjusted. To alter the depth of a section of the form:

1 move the pointer to the bottom edge of the section, where it will change shape ‡ ;

2 drag down to increase the depth of the section.

To alter the area of the form, drag the right and bottom edges to the size that you require.

Task 1: Customising the membership form

The aim of this task is to create the form shown in FIGURE 14.1. Exact instructions are not given because you can experiment with selecting and moving controls. You may find it useful to widen the form temporarily so that controls can be moved to temporary positions while you rearrange them on the form. If you wish to keep a group of controls together, select them as a group and then they can be moved as a group. Also try aligning groups of controls to achieve a tidy looking form.

1 Open the Membership form in design view.

2 Try to create the form shown in FIGURE 14.1. If you inadvertently delete a field from the form, see the following table for instructions on how to restore it.

3 When you have rearranged the detail section save the form design using **File-Save**.

Deleting or restoring fields from or to a form

To...	Do this
Delete a label or label text box	Select the control and press *Delete* or use **Edit-Delete** to delete both label and entry box. To delete only the label click on it again before deleting.
	Note: if you delete a field you will not be able to use the form to enter data into this field. Use **Edit-Undo** if you unintentionally delete a field.
Restore a label and field	Use **View-Field List** to display the list of fields available in the table. Click on the field name required and drag to the required position on the form. If the form is a single-column form then both label and field will appear, although the label will require editing. If the form is a tabular one then just the field will be restored.

Changing the text of a field name label

The text of a field name label may be edited and, if required, additional text can be added to the form.

To...	Do this
Add a label	Click on the Label tool in the Toolbox window (see FIGURE 21.1), click on the form in the required position and type the text required.
Edit a label	Double-click on the label to display an insertion point in the text. Edit the text as required. Press *Enter* or click on a blank part of the form when finished.

Altering the size and font of controls

To alter the size or font of controls in a form:

1 Select the control(s) to be altered.

2 Open the font list box in the toolbar and select the font required.

3 Open the point size list box and select the point size required.

4 Click on the left, centre or right alignment button on the toolbar.

Note: if you increase the size of a font you may need to alter the size of the control and the size of the section.

Task 2: Adding text to the form header

In this task text is added to the header section of the **Membership** form.

1 Open the **Membership** form in design mode.

2 Widen the Form Header section.

3 Click on the Label tool in the Toolbox window.

4 Click in the space created for the form header and key in the text *Chelmer Leisure and Recreation Centre*.

5 Drag the label to be larger and increase the size of this text.
   You may wish to change the font.

6 Move and size the heading as in FIGURE 14.1, and add the text *Membership Application Form*.
   If you wish you may alter the font or size of this text.

7 Save the form.

Task 3: Using the customised form to enter data

To gain a full appreciation of the modifications made to the **Membership** form, it should be used to enter data.

1 Open the form from the Database window by clicking on the **Open** button.

2 Move through the records and display a blank form.

3 Compose data for a new member and, using the form, enter data into the next record.

4 Close the form.

Reorganising the field order

When data is entered into each field, Enter or Tab takes you to the next field. The order in which the fields are entered is defined by the order in which they were selected in the Form Wizard. Once the form has been modified then this order may need to be changed. To change the tab order of the fields:

1 From the design view, choose **View-Tab Order** to display the **Tab Order** dialog box (FIGURE 15.4). This dialog box displays the order of the fields in the **Custom Order** box. In the **Section** box normally the Detail section is selected.

2 To alter the order of the fields select the field or fields to be moved and drag to the new position to achieve the new order.

3 When the new order has been selected click on **OK**.

FIGURE 15.4

The **Auto Order** button will set the tab order according to the way in which the fields are set out on the form; fields are ordered with the priority of left to right and then top to bottom.

Adding headers and footers

It is straightforward to add text into the header and footer sections of a form. Headers and footers are always displayed on the screen. Calculated text may be added to the header or the footer; for example, the date can be shown.

If a form is to be printed the header section prints before the first record and the footer section prints after the last record. Extra sections, page header and page footer can be added, which will print on each page of the printout. You can control whether to display or print these sections. Calculated text may be added to show the page numbers. Page breaks may occur in the middle of records, if the record is in single-column format. This can be avoided by adjusting the Keep Together setting of the Detail properties from No to Yes. To display the Properties sheet check that the **Properties** button is depressed and click on the Detail bar.

Task 4: Adding the date

The aim of this task is to put the date in the **Membership Category** form footer.

1 Open the **Membership Category** form in design view.

2 Click on the **Text Box** tool in the Toolbox.

3   Click on the form footer bar and choose **Insert-Date and Time**. Select a suitable date format and click on **OK** .

4   Switch to run mode by clicking on the Form View button to see the result.

5   Close the form.

Task 5: Adding headers and footers to a printed form

When a form is printed the header is printed at the beginning and the footer is printed at the end of the records. To add a header and footer that print at the top of each page of the **Membership** form when printed:

1   Open the **Membership** form.

2   Click on the **Print Preview** button.

3   Close the preview and display the form in design view.

4   Choose **View-Page Header/Footer**.
    Two extra sections appear, Page Header and Page Footer.

5   Select all the title in the form header and use **Edit-Copy**.

6   Click on the Page Header bar and use **Edit-Paste**. Position the pasted copy.

7   Click on the Page Footer bar and choose **Insert-Page Number**. Choose a suitable format and click on **OK** .

8   Click on the Form Header bar. Display the Properties sheet by clicking on the Properties button on the toolbar.

9   In the Section properties box select the **All** tab and click in the **Display When** box.

10 Open the list and select Screen Only.

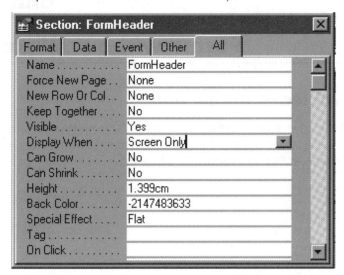

11 Click on the Detail bar and change the Keep Together property to Yes to prevent page breaks in the middle of records.

12 Preview and print the form.

Forms without Wizards

What you will learn in this unit

The previous units have considered creating forms using the Form Wizard. This method may be restricting when creating a custom form, and forms may be created without using the Wizard. In this unit you will see how to:

- open a blank form

- choose the type of form

- add controls to the form.

Creating a blank form

If the columnar or tabular layout is not suitable for the intended form, then it may be easier to start with a blank form and create a custom design.

Choosing the type of form

If a form is created using AutoForm or the Form Wizard you are given the choice of the type of form. If a blank form is chosen then only a blank detail section is displayed. To create a blank form and choose its type:

1 Click on the Form tab in the Database window, click on the **New** button, and highlight Design View.

2 Select the table upon which the form is to be based and click on **OK**.

3 Choose **Edit-Select Form** to display the Form Properties sheet.

4 Look at the Default View property. This should be set at Single Form.

Adding header/footer sections

Choose **View-Form Header/Footer** to add the header/footer sections to the form. If you intend to print the form then page header/footer sections may also be added.

Adding a label to the form

A label is the simplest control that you can add to your form. Labels are unbound (see Unit 21); they only display the text which you give to them. Labels may be added anywhere in the form, for example, as a title in the header section. To add a label to a form:

1 Click on the label button on the toolbox. Position the pointer in the form at the point where the label should go. The pointer becomes a symbol with two parts, the label symbol and the cross-hair symbol used for box drawing.

2 Either click to put a small label box on the workspace which will expand as you add text, or by dragging draw a box of the desired size. If you drag below the bottom or to the right of the particular section, this part of the form will expand to accommodate the size of label you require.

3 The label is outlined and inside it a flashing insertion point appears, ready for you to enter text. If you don't enter any text and click the mouse button the label will disappear.

4 The size and font may be adjusted by selecting the label and formatting using the appropriate list boxes in the toolbar.

Adding a text box

A text box is the most common type of control that is found on forms. The fields to which text boxes can be bound will be found in the field list which is compiled from the source table or query. To add a text box:

1 To display the field list window, click on the Field List button on the toolbar or choose **View-Field List**. Choose **View-Grid** to put a matrix of lines on the form to help with positioning the controls. Note that this grid is not visible when the form is run.

2 Click on the required field in the field list and, holding down the mouse button, drag to the Detail workspace. While pointing in the workspace the pointer becomes a field symbol. The position of the field symbol indicates the upper left-hand corner of the text box, not the label, so position the top left corner to allow room to the left for the label.

3 Click to place the label and field boxes. Position them by using the hand symbol to drag or by dragging the anchor handle, and size by using one of the sizing handles.

4 If desired, select the size and font of the text in the control.

5 More than one field may be selected from the field list, and multiple fields can be placed as a group. To select a contiguous selection click on the first field and hold down the *Shift* key while clicking on the last field in the group. To select a non-contiguous selection hold down the *Control* key while making the selection.

6 The order in which the fields are selected determines the 'tab order', i.e. the order in which they will be filled in on the form. If this needs amending, then from the form design screen choose **View-Tab Order**. In the dialog box use a drag and drop method to rearrange the order of the fields.

Adding a multi-line text box

Multi-line text boxes are usually used to display memo fields. They are larger than the single line boxes. They also have a vertical scroll bar (visible when the control is selected while the form is being run) so that when there is too much text to be fitted into the text box then the scroll bar can be used to move through the text.

1 From the field list select a memo field. Drag the field list pointer to the lower middle part of the detail section and drop.

2 Adjust the size of the text box and position the label.

103

3 Display the Format category of the Text Box properties window until you see the Scroll Bars property box appear. You should see Vertical for this property, which adds a vertical scroll bar to your text box. Note that the scroll bar will only appear when you click in the text box while the form is run, indicating to Access that you are using this control.

4 You may wish to print the form, so to make sure that the whole memo field is printed, in the Properties window, change both the Can Grow and the Can Shrink properties to Yes. This will not affect the text box while it is being displayed on the screen.

Task 1: Creating a blank form

Although forms have been created either using AutoForm or FormWizard, this task will explore using a blank form which will duplicate one of the forms already created. The table that is to be used is the **Membership** table.

1 Click on the Form tab in the Database window, and highlight Design View. Select the **Membership** table and click on **OK**.

2 Access creates a new form, showing the detail section.

3 In the Form Properties box, if necessary, change the default view property to Single Form.

4 Add a header and footer section by choosing **View-Form Header/Footer**.
You should see a matrix of lines on the form's workspace; if not then select **View-Grid** to display it.

5 Adjust the depth of the detail section by pointing to the top line of the Form Footer bar.
The pointer should change shape to a horizontal bar with a double-headed arrow. Click and drag downward to expand the detail section area.

6 Add all of the fields, by clicking and dragging from the field list.
Consider the order in which you select and place them. Try selecting and placing a group of fields.

7 Add a title to the form and save the form as **Membership 2**.
Remember that there is a distinction between the title of the form and the name it is saved under.

8 Run the form and use it to add another record to the **Membership** table.

9 If the order of field entry does not match the form design, for instance if the fields were not selected in the right order, then the order can be changed by returning to design view and choosing **View-Tab Order**. Save the changes.

Forms design: integrative tasks

The following tasks revise some of the topics covered in this and the previous two units.

Task 2: Designing and using forms

There are two other tables that require forms to be designed, the **Classes** table and the **Bookings** table.

1   Use AutoForm and Form Wizard to create columnar forms for both these tables, saving them as **Classes** and **Bookings**, respectively.

2   Use the forms to enter the data for these tables shown in Quick Reference 2.

Remind yourself of the validation rules set in Unit 9 and try testing them while entering the data.

3   Close the forms when the data has been entered.

Task 3: Adding a new table and creating a form

This task recaps on some of the activities met during these first three sessions. The aim of this activity is to create a new table and link it to the Chelmer database and create a form to input data into this table. The table to be created is the **Tutor** table.

The **Tutor** table could comprise the following fields: **Lastname, Initials, Title, Street, Town, County, Post Code, Telephone No, National Insurance No, Date of Birth** and **Qualifications**. Create this **Tutor** table, make all fields text and choose suitable lengths for each, except for **Date of Birth** and **Qualifications**. Use a short date for **Date of Birth** and a memo for **Qualifications**. Save the table as **Tutor**. Create a link between this table and the **Classes** table using **View-Relationships**.

Use **Relationships-Show Table** to add the **Tutor** table. Drag the field **Lastname** from the **Tutors** table (the 'one' side of the relationship) to the **Class Tutor** found in the **Classes** table (the 'many' side of the relationship).

Consider the pros and cons of checking the **Enforce Referential Integrity** check box. If there is no data in the **Tutor** table you will not be able to enforce referential integrity.

To design a form for this table:

1   Select the Form tab in the Database window, then click on the ▮New▮ button.

2   Select Design View for the **Tutor** table.
    Access creates a new form, showing the Detail section.

3   Inspect the **Form Properties** box to see that the Default View property is Single Form.

4   Add a header and footer section by choosing **View-Form Header/Footer**.
    You should see a matrix of lines on the form's workspace. If not, then select **View-Grid** to display it.

5   Adjust the depth of the detail section by pointing to the top line of the Form Footer bar.
    The pointer should change shape to a horizontal bar with double headed arrow. Click and drag downward to expand the detail section area.

6   Add all the fields to the form from the field list

7   Add a title to the form and save the form as *Tutor*.

8   Select the text box for qualifications so that its properties sheet is displayed. Set the following properties for this text box: Scroll bars – Vertical, Can Shrink – Yes, Can Grow – Yes.

9   Save the form and run it.

10 Use it to enter the following tutor record: Evans, P J, Mrs, 25 Lyme Green, Chelmer, Cheshire, CH2 1ED, 0777 560935, XZ 32 99 06B, 17/7/70, Y.M C. A. Dance to Music, Certificate in Aerobics, First Aid (Red Cross).

Task 4: Adding text to a form

Add some text to the **Membership** form next to the Sex check box to inform the user of the form that a tick indicates male and blank indicates female.

Using Report Wizard and AutoReport

What you will learn in this unit

This unit explores the basic design of printed reports that include data from an Access table. It explains how to create a report quickly using Report Wizard. Later units develop some of the themes in this unit more fully. At the end of this unit you will be able to:

■ create a report using Report Wizard or AutoReport

■ save and close a report

■ use a report to print data from an Access table.

Reports are used to print information from a number of records. Reports can show the data from either a table or a query. In addition to records, they may show summary information relating to the records displayed. Graphs created using Microsoft Graph may be added to reports.

Reports, then, are intended to allow you to select the data to be printed and then to present that data in an acceptable format. To emphasise the distinction between reports and forms: reports are intended to be printed, while screen forms are normally displayed on screen (although the facilities often also exist for printing them).

In most applications you will create a number of different standard reports. For example, a mailing list of clients may simply show customer name and address, but a list showing outstanding orders to specific clients will also show details of the items that customers have ordered, their value and other associated information.

Access allows you to create reports either to your own design using its wide range of tools for customising reports, or to start by using Report Wizard which provides you quickly and easily with a basic report, which you can later format and customise. We use Report Wizard here because it allows you to understand the basic concept of what a report is and how it works, before you grapple with customising specific features of the report.

Since forms and reports share many design and creation features, you will reuse some of the skills that you acquired earlier in designing a form to help you to design a report.

Creating a single-column report with Report Wizard

There are various types of report that can be created with Report Wizard. First we deal with the single-column report, which is used most frequently and is relatively simple to create. A single-column report places all of the selected fields in a single column, with their field names to the left.

1 To enter Report Wizard starting from the Database window, either click on New in the Database window when you are displaying reports, or click the New Object button on the toolbar and select New Report. A New Report dialog box appears (FIGURE 17.1).

FIGURE 17.1

2 Select the Report Wizard option to create a report using Report Wizard.

3 Click on the down arrow button of the 'Choose the table or query...' list box to produce a list of tables and queries, and select the table for which you wish to create a report.

4 Click on OK.

5   The next stage is to choose which fields are to be in the report. The fields that you can have in the report are shown in the **Available Fields** box (FIGURE 17.2).

FIGURE 17.2

6   These can be transferred to the report by selecting each field in turn and clicking on the [>] button.

7   If you wish to add all of the fields in the table to the report then click on the [>>] button.

8   You may set the order in which the fields appear on the report by selecting them in the order that you desire. The [<] button will remove a highlighted field from a report and [<<] will remove all of the fields from the report.

9   Once you have added the required fields to the report continue by clicking on the Next> button.

10 The next dialog box asks you to indicate grouping levels. Leave this for now and click on the Next> button. We shall return to this in Unit 18.

11 The next dialog box asks you to select the order in which records will be sorted (FIGURE 17.3). Select the fields you want the records to be sorted by. If you have only a small set of records, just one sort field will be adequate. If you want records to appear in the same order as in the table or query it is not necessary to indicate a sort field. Choose the Next> button.

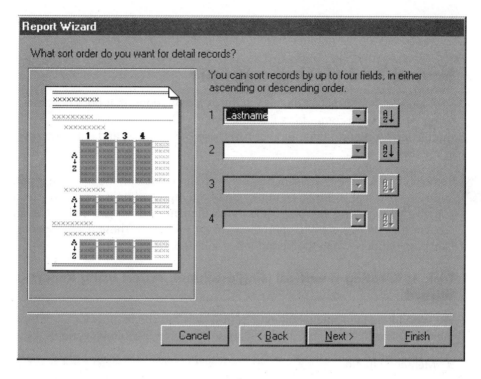

FIGURE 17.3

12 The next dialog box concerns itself with the layout of the printout on the paper and whether the report is to be in portrait or landscape orientation. The choice of layout depends on whether or not grouping is used. On the first occasion choose Vertical and Portrait. Click on Next>.

13 You are then asked what kind of style you want for your form. You are given a choice of:

- Bold

- Casual

- Compact

- Corporate

- Formal

- Soft Gray

14 The style decides the appearance of the field names and field contents in the report. An example of the style is shown on the left of the dialog box. Click on each style in turn to see what it would look like. On the first occasion a report is created choose Corporate. The style can be modified later. Click on the Next> button.

15 The next thing that you are asked for is a title. Enter a report title. Report titles are particularly important in flagging the purpose of the report to the reader, so choose something that conveys the contents of the report.

16 With the 'Preview the report' option selected, click on **Finish** . Note that Access
has added a page number and the date at the bottom of every page.

Saving and closing a report

Save a report by choosing **File-Save**. If this is a new report that does not have a
name, Access will prompt for a filename with a **File-Save As** dialog box. If you later
want to save a report under another name use **File-Save As**, and enter the new name
in the dialog box.

Remember that there is a distinction between the name and the title of a report. The
title is the text that is displayed at the top of the report when it is printed. The name
you give when saving the form is the form's filename, which you need to be able to
recognise when you want to open the form for use again. These names appear in the
Database window when the Report tab is selected.

Task 1: Creating a vertical (single-column) report using Report Wizard

We wish to create a single-column report which lists the records for all of the
members who have records in the database, showing the following fields:

- **Membership No**
- **Category No**
- **Firstname**
- **Lastname**
- **Occupation**
- **Date of Birth**
- **Sporting Interests**

We wish to create a report that looks like the extract shown below:

Chelmer Leisure and Recreation Centre Members

Membership No	1
Category No	2
Firstname	Andrew J
Lastname	Walker
Occupation	Builder
Date of birth	12/3/52
Sporting Interests	Tennis, squash
Membership No	2
Category No	1
Firstname	Denise
Lastname	Cartwright

1   To enter Report Wizard starting from the Database window, click on New in the Database window when you are displaying reports, or click the New Object button on the toolbar and select New Report.
    A **New Report** dialog box appears.

2   Select the **Report Wizard** option to create a report using Report Wizard.

3   Click on the down arrow button of the 'Choose the table or query...' list box, to produce a list of tables and queries and select the **Membership** table. Click on OK .

4   Select the fields to appear in the report by clicking on the field names above in the **Available Fields** list box, and then clicking on the > button. The selected fields should appear in the **Selected Fields** list box.

    If any fields are included by mistake, use < to remove them. Choose Next> .

5   Do not indicate a grouping level.

    If Access has automatically created one (on Category No) then click on < to remove the grouping. Click on the Next> button.

6   Choose to sort by Membership No by entering it in the first box. Choose Next>.

7   Choose Vertical and Portrait for the report layout.

8   Choose Corporate for the style of the report. Choose Next> .

9   Enter the following report title: *Chelmer Leisure and Recreation Centre Members*.

10 With the option Preview the report selected, click on Finish to display the report on the screen.

11 Access will automatically save the report with the name *Chelmer Leisure and Recreation Centre Members*.

Using a report

To use a report, first display the available report names in the Database window, then double-click on the report name and the Print Preview window will appear, showing a preview of how the report will appear when printed. Alternatively, click on the report name and then click on the Preview button.

To zoom in and out and to view a complete page on the screen, click on the report.

Note that a report picks up the table properties of the table or query that the report used when it was designed. Later, you change the properties of the table or query without changing the properties of the report.

Printing a report

Before printing any report always view the report in Print Preview.

Previewing

To preview a report:

1 Click the **Preview** button, and a miniature version of what is to be printed will be displayed.

2 To zoom in and zoom out simply click anywhere on the preview, or use the zoom button. Click on the **Zoom** Control box to select a specific magnification for the preview.

3 Choose **File-Page Setup** to make adjustments such as the orientation (portrait or landscape), the choice of printer and the width of the margins. Some of the options in the **Page Setup** dialog box will be familiar since you will have used them in printing tables and queries, but there are also special options for use when printing a report, such as the number of items (records) across the page, item size and item layout. Click on **OK** when the required adjustments have been made.

Printing

When you are satisfied that the preview is correct, printing may be done from either the preview screen or the design screen. To print from the preview screen:

1 Click on the **Print** button in the Print Preview bar.

2 Select whether all or certain pages of the report will be printed and the number of copies. Click on **OK** .

Alternatively, to print from the design screen:

1 Choose **File-Print**.

2 Select whether all or certain pages of the report will be printed and the number of copies. Click on **OK** .

Task 2: Using and printing a report

To use the report **Chelmer Leisure and Recreation Centre Members**, first select it from the filenames displayed in the Database window, by double clicking on the report name. The Print Preview window will appear, showing a preview of how the report will appear when printed.

Now print the report:

1 Choose **File-Page Setup**.

Now experiment with different setup options, as follows.

2 Two items across the page, by entering *2* in the **Items Across** box.

You may need to adjust the width in the Item Size section to less than half your page width.

3   With two items across the page, explore the effect of Down, then Across and Across, then Down in the Layout Items section.

4   Try making item Height larger.

5   Close the **Print Setup** dialog box between each trial in order to view the new layout in Print Preview.

6   When you have a layout with which you are happy, print it, by selecting the **Print** button.

Creating a report using AutoReport

The really easy way to create a report is to allow Access to do all of the work for you, by using AutoReport. This, however, does not allow any scope for specifying the contents or style of the report.

To use AutoReport:

1 Click on the **Report** tab in the Database window, then the **New** button.

2 In the **New Report** dialog box select either AutoReport: Columnar or AutoReport: Tabular.

3 Click on the down arrow button of the 'Choose the table or query...' list box, to produce a list of tables and queries, and select the table for which you wish to create a report.

4 Click on **OK** and the report will be created and displayed on the screen.

5 Use **File-Save** and give the report a name.

Task 3: Creating a tabular report using AutoReport

This task demonstrates how easy it is to create a report using AutoReport.

1   Click on the **Reports** tab and the **New** button.

2   In the **New Report** dialog box select AutoReport: Tabular.

3   Click on the down arrow button of the 'Choose the table or query...' list box and select the table **Membership Category**.

4   Click on **OK** and the report will be created and displayed on the screen in preview mode.

5   Save it as ***Membership Category*** and print this report.

Grouped reports

What you will learn in this unit

This unit explores the creation of reports where records are arranged in groups according to the value of fields in a table or query. At the end of this unit you will be able to:

■ create a report with grouped records

Note: you may choose to omit this unit for the moment and return to it later when you are ready to design this kind of report.

Understanding grouped reports

A grouped report puts the fields you select into a row and groups the records according to the value of a field in the table or query. This approach can also be used simply to create a report in a table form with fields shown in columns, if you do not specify groups. The advantage of this type of report is that it displays more records to the page. However, it does not display records with several long fields, which therefore cannot be accommodated next to each other on the page in parallel columns.

Records can be grouped by several different fields, although we shall use only one field for grouping.

Apart from the need to define how records will be displayed in groups, the process of creating a groups/totals report is similar to that for a single-column report. The process is basically:

1 Select the fields to appear in the report.

2 Select how the records in the table or query will be grouped for the report. Groups are divisions within a report that include all records that have a value for a specific field.

3 Select the order in which you want the groups created (if you are using more than one group).

4 Select how the records are to be sorted for the report.

5 Select a layout for the report.

6 Select a style for the report.

7 Add the report's title.

8 Use Print Preview to display the report on screen.

9 Save the report.

10 Print the report, as appropriate, and subsequently close the report.

Task 1: Creating a grouped report using Report Wizard

We wish to create a grouped report which lists all the members for which there are records in the database, showing the following fields:

- **Category No**
- **Lastname**
- **Firstname**
- **Telephone No**

The records are to be grouped according to Category No, so that, for instance, all records with a given Category No are grouped together. We wish to create a report that looks like the one shown below.

Members by Membership Category

Category No	Lastname	Firstname	Telephone No
1			
	Barrett	Martha A	01777 557822
	Cartwright	Denise	01777 552099
	Davies	Sandra M	01778 891441
	Jameson	Donna	
	Jones	Edward R	01777 567333
	Robinson	Rebecca	01777 568812
	Weiner	George W F	
2			
	Everett	Alan	
	Forsythe	Ann M	01777 569945
	Shangali	Imran	01777 561553

1 Enter Report Wizard by clicking the **New** button in the Database window with the Reports tab selected.

2 Click on the **Report Wizard** option to create a report using Report Wizard.

3 From the 'Choose the table or query...' drop-down list box, select the **Membership** table. Click on **OK** .

4 Select the fields to appear in the report by clicking on the field names as indicated above, in the **Available Fields** list box, and then clicking on the button.

The selected fields should appear in the **Selected Fields** list box. If any fields are included by mistake use to remove them.

5 Click on Next>.

You will probably discover that Access has automatically grouped the records by Category No. If not, click on **Category No** in the list of fields and then click on to display it in the heading box in the preview. Click on Next>

6 Sort records within groups alphabetically by the **Lastname** field. Choose Next>.

7 Select Stepped and Portrait for the layout of the report. Choose Next>.

8 Select Compact for the style of the report. Choose Next>.

9 Enter the following report title: *Members by Membership Category*.

10 Choose 'Preview the report' and click on <kbd>Finish</kbd>.

As the wizard was used to create the report it is automatically saved with the name of its title, i.e. **Members by Membership Category**.

11 To print the report directly, click on the **Print** button. To change print options display the Print dialog box using File-Print and make the choices you require before clicking on <kbd>OK</kbd>.

Task 2: Creating a grouped report using more than one group

In this task a grouped report is created that lists all of the members for whom there are records in the database, showing the following fields:

- **Category No**
- **Lastname**
- **Firstname**
- **Town**
- **Telephone No**

The records are to be grouped according to **Category No** and **Town**, so that all records with a given **Category No** are grouped together and within this grouping all records with a given **Town** will be grouped together. We wish to create a report which looks like the one shown below.

Membership by Membership Category and Town

Category No	Town	Lastname	Firstname	Telephone No
1				
	Chelmer			
		Jameson	Donna	
		Jones	Edward R	01777 567333
		Robinson	Rebecca	01777 568812
		Weiner	George W F	
	Meirton			
		Barrett	Martha A	01777 557822
		Cartwright	Denise	01777 552099
		Davies	Sandra M	01778 891441

1 Follow the first five steps as for Task 1.

You will probably discover that Access has automatically grouped the records by Category No. If not click on **Category No** in the list of fields and then click on

 to display it in the heading box in the preview.

2   To add **Town** to the grouping select it and click on [>]. Click on [Next>].

3   Sort records within groups alphabetically by the **Lastname** field. Choose [Next>].

4   Select Stepped and Portrait for the Layout of the report. Choose [Next>].

5   Select Compact for the style of the report. Choose [Next>].

6   Enter the following report title: **Members by Membership Category and Town**.

7   Choose 'Preview the report' and click on [Finish].
    As the Wizard was used to create the report it is automatically saved with the name of its title, i.e. **Members by Membership Category and Town**.

8   To print the report directly, click on the [Print] button. To change print options, display the **Print** dialog box using **File-Print** and make the choices you require before clicking on [OK].

Task 3: Selecting the order of grouping

1   Create a report that is the same as the one in Task 2, with the records grouped according to Category No and Town.
    This time show all records with a given Town grouped together and within this grouping show all records with a given Category No grouped together.

2   Create this report as in Task 2, and when you have added Town as a grouping, click on the Priority up arrow to change the priority of grouping.

3   Continue as before but title this report *Members by Town and Membership Category*.
    Note the difference between this report and the previous one.

Mailing label reports

What you will learn in this unit

Mailing label reports allow the creation of mailing labels, from, say, a table of names and addresses. A mailing label report fits the fields you select into a rectangle that is designed to print labels. Unlike other Report Wizard reports, this type does not show field names. It does, however, make it easy to add text such as commas and spaces.

At the end of this unit you will be able to:

■ create a mailing label report

■ use a query in the process of creating a Report Wizard report

■ perform a mail merge to create an accompanying letter.

Creating a mailing label report

The procedure for creating a mailing label report is similar to that for creating any other type of report, except that you use a special Label Wizard.

To create a mailing label report:

1 With Reports displayed in the Database window, select New .

2 Click on the Label Wizard option and select a table or query to provide the data for the labels report. Click on OK to display the first of the Label Wizard dialog boxes (FIGURE 19.1).

FIGURE 19.1

3 Select the size of labels from the list. Label sizes are listed according to their Avery number. If you do not know the Avery label number for a given label size, look at the Dimensions and Number across columns to find the label size that matches your labels.

4 Select Unit of Measure and Label Type and click on Next> .

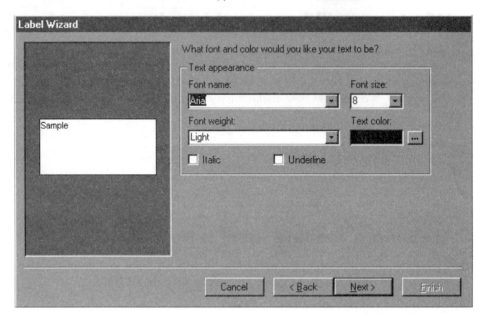

FIGURE 19.2

5 Select the Font name, Font size, Font weight and Text color. You may also check Italic and/or Underline. Click on Next> .

6 Select fields as with other report types, so that they appear on the prototype label, but remember that more than one field can be added to a line.

7 Add text, fields and punctuation to a line and then advance to a new line by pressing *Enter* (FIGURE 19.3). When you have created the label, click on Next> .

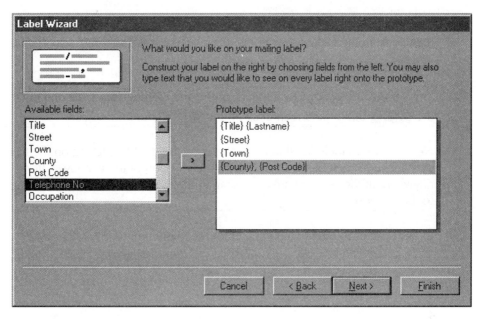

FIGURE 19.3

8   Select how the records are to be sorted, or in other words the order in which mailing labels are to be printed. Click on **Next>** .

9   Either accept the name for the report or type in a name for it. With 'See the mailing labels as they will look printed' selected, click on **Finish** to display the labels on screen.

10 Save the report.

11 Print and close the report as appropriate.

Task 1: Creating a mailing label Report Wizard report based on a query

We wish to create a mailing label report which lists all members who joined since 1/1/95. An extract from such a report is shown below. First we need to define and execute a query to select the appropriate records, and then we need to define the mailing label report that is to be used to display this set of records.

Mr Gray	Miss Robinson
4 The Parade	16 Lowton Lane
Chelmer	Branford
Cheshire, CH1 7ER	Staffs, ST10 2DZ

Query design and execution were introduced earlier, and you may wish to review this topic at this point.

To define the query:

1   Starting from the Database window, click on the **Queries** tab, and click on the
    New button to create a new query.

2   The **Show Table** dialog box appears. Select the **Membership** table and click on
    the **Add** button and then click on the **Close** button.

3   Next choose to include all fields in the query by double-clicking on the title bar
    of the field list box of the table in the upper section of the window. Click
    anywhere in the selected area and drag to the field row to transfer all of the fields
    to the lower section.

4   In the **Date of Joining** criteria cell enter the query criteria *>1/1/95*.
    To view the result of this query click on the **Query View** button on the toolbar.

5   Save the query by choosing **File-Save**.

6   In the **Query Name** box of the **Save As** dialog box, enter the query name: *New
    Members*.

7   Close the query.

Now that you have defined a query, you need to design a report to display the
records retrieved by the query:

8   Click on the **Reports** tab in the Database window and click on **New** .

9   Select the **Label Wizard** option to create a report using Label Wizard.

10 From the 'Choose the table or query…' drop-down list box, select the query New
    Members. Click on **OK** .

11 Select the size of the labels. Click on **Next>** .
    You may need to experiment with different label sizes. Try Avery number L7160 first.

12 Leave the font as default and click on **Next>** .

13 The fields to be included are, in order, as follows:

    ■ **Title**

    ■ **Lastname**

    ■ **Street**

    ■ **Town**

    ■ **County**

    ■ **Post Code**

14 Add the field **Title** followed by a space and then the field **Lastname** to the first line. Press the *Enter* button to move onto the next line.

15 Add **Street** to the next line.

16 Add the remainder of the fields, each to a separate line, with the exception of **County** and **Post Code**, which should be on the same line separated by a comma and a space. Click on **Next>** .

17 Choose to order the records according to **Lastname**.

18 Accept the title *Labels New Members*. The report is automatically saved.

19 With 'See the labels…' selected, click on **Finish** to display the report on the screen.

20 To print the report directly select the **Print** button. To display the **Print** dialog box use **File-Print**.

Mail merging

When a circular is to be sent out, creating mailing labels takes the tedium out of addressing the envelopes. The process can be further automated by using Access in conjunction with Word to perform a mail merge. In Word a standard letter can be produced and Access can provide the data (usually names and addresses) to be merged with the standard letter.

Task 2: Mail merging

For this task you will need both Access and Word. A standard letter is to be sent to all of the fitness instructors telling them of the times of opening over the Easter holiday. If you have not already done so you will need to complete, say, four records in the **Tutor** table (the names of the fitness instructors are in the **Classes** table).

1 With the **Tables** tab selected, highlight the **Tutor** table in the Database window.

2 Open the OfficeLinks drop-down list (on the toolbar) and select Merge It.

3 Choose the option to create a new document and click on **OK**.

This causes Word to be loaded in mail merge mode. Note: ensure that there is data in at least one tutor record otherwise this will not work.

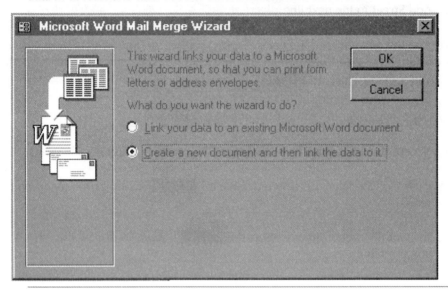

4 Next create a standard letter, as illustrated below.

The parts of the letter that are replaceable fields are shown enclosed in double chevrons. To insert a replaceable field click on the **Insert Merge Field** button on the mail merge toolbar and select the required field from the drop-down list.

Chelmer Leisure and Recreation Centre

Tel: 01777 563444

Park View Road

Fax: 01777 560112

Chelmer

Cheshire

CE9 1JS

19 March, 1997

<<Street>>

<<Town>>

<<County>>

<<Post Code>>

Dear <<Title>> <<Surname>>

Please note the following times when the Centre will be open during the Easter break.

Good Friday	9:00am to 5:00pm
Easter Saturday	9:00am to 1:00pm
Easter Sunday	Closed
Easter Monday	9:00am to 5pm
Tuesday	Normal hours

If you wish to reschedule any classes please let me know as soon as possible.

Yours sincerely

G V Richards

Manager

5 It is best to check the merge for errors first. Do this by clicking on the `Check for Errors` button and selecting the 'Simulate the merge ...' option. If the merge was successful then no errors will be reported and you may continue by either merging to the printer or to a file.

6 To complete the task, design a mailing label report to accompany the letters produced.

Customising a report

What you will learn in this unit

This unit explores some of the basic tools for designing customised reports instead of using the standard reports that can be created using the Report Wizard.

At the end of this unit you will be able to:

- appreciate the component parts of a report
- create a blank report as a basis for later design work
- move and size controls
- change the reports area
- delete, add and restore fields to a report
- change the text of a field name
- add headers and footers.

Understanding customised reports

Although Report Wizard produces a useful basic report, eventually you may wish to design or create your own from scratch, so that you can exercise greater control over the report design. If you examine the Report Wizard reports that you have created recently you will note that they have the following limitations: the title length is restricted; the spacing is fixed horizontal spacing, which makes it difficult to distinguish between records; and the fixed format gives the same standard appearance time and time again.

This unit explores some of the simple tools for customising a report. These may be applied either to a report created initially with Report Wizard, or to create your own report independently. Before attempting to create or modify a report, it is useful to identify the components of a report. These are listed and described below. If you examine the reports that you have just created using Report Wizard, you should recognise that they have these components. If you display an existing report in Design view, by clicking on the **Design** button with the report selected in the Database window, the report will be displayed with these areas clearly marked.

Components of a report

Component	Description
Report header	contains any headings or other introductory text that might appear at the beginning of the report.
Page header	contains headings that will appear at the top of each page, such as a running title and page numbers.
Detail	shows data from the records in the database. Sets up the format for records in general, which is then used for every record to be included in the report
Page footer	appears at the bottom of the page.
Report footer	contains information at the end of the report, such as a final summary or a statement, e.g. 'this is the end of the report'.
Group header	marks the beginning of a group; usually introduces the group that the report will display.
Group footer	marks the end of a group and often contains sections that summarise the records that are part of a group.

Working with report design allows you to adjust the contents, size and position of everything that appears in the report. As with forms, each small piece of a report is called a control. Controls include fields, data, text, picture and calculations. Again, many of the features relating to forms that you experimented with earlier also apply to reports.

Modifying an existing report

To customise an existing report it must be selected in Design mode, thus:

1 Select the report in the Database window and then select the **Design** button, or

2 Click on the report name using the right mouse button and choose **Design** from the shortcut menu.

Creating a new blank report

To create a new report, without the aid of Report Wizard:

1 Click on the **Reports** tab in the Database window and on **New**, or

2 Choose **View-Database Objects-Reports** and then click on the **New** button in the Database window, or

3 Click on the drop-down **New Object** button on the toolbar, then select New Report.

4 Select the Design View option in the **New Report** dialog box to create a report without using Report Wizard.

5 Click on the down arrow button of the 'Choose the table or query...' list box to produce a list of tables and queries, and select the table for which you wish to create a report.

6 Click on **OK**.

Extra windows

When you create a new blank report the Toolbox window will be displayed. This is useful for adding controls to the report. There are a number of such windows which you will encounter as you advance in report design. These are:

Window	Description
Properties sheet	to change different features of the report's contents
Field list	to add controls bound to fields
Toolbox	to select the design tool required (it can be dragged to the left of the screen, where it 'locks' as a toolbar)

All of these windows can be moved or closed in the same way as any other window. They can also be opened and closed from the **View** menu.

Task 1: Examining the components of a report

1   Examine one of the reports that you have created with the Report Wizard.

2   With the Database window displayed, click on Report, and then **Design** .
Note that Report Wizard creates reports with default settings in many areas.

3   Examine the report that you have displayed. Click on each control in turn. What are the default settings for the following?

- Page header

- Report header

- Detail

- Report footer

- Page footer

- Group header

- Group footer

Task 2: Creating a blank report

Create a blank report for the **Classes** table, showing all of the fields in the table, thus:

1   Click on the **Reports** tab in the Database window, and then click the **New** button in the Database window.

2   Select the **Classes** table from the 'Choose the table or query...' drop-down list box.

3   Select the Design View option.

4   Consider the layout and decide where to put title, field labels and the fields themselves.

5   Add all of the fields to the report from the field list. Display the field list and double-click on the Field List title bar to highlight all the fields.

6   Click and drag the highlighted fields onto the Detail section of the report. Controls for all the fields should appear.

7   Save as **Classes** and close.

Moving and sizing controls

Moving and sizing controls is the basic activity for improving the appearance of the report.

In order to move a control, the control must first be selected and then it can be moved by dragging it. The different types of controls can be selected in the same way as controls are selected and moved on forms. If you need a reminder, see the section on 'Moving and sizing controls' in Unit 15.

Task 3: Moving and sizing controls on an existing Report Wizard report

We wish to improve on the design of the report **Members**, so that the final report looks like this:

1   First open the existing report. Select the report **Members** in the Database window and then select the ▐ Design ▌ button.

2   Now move the controls on the report until it resembles the Design screen shown above, using the instructions above for selecting and moving controls.

If the toolbox is in the way, remove it by using **View-Toolbox.**

You may get into a muddle in your first attempt to move controls. Remember that controls can be deleted by selecting them and using the *Delete* key. If all else fails close without saving and start again.

3   View the new report on screen using **Print Preview**

4   Save the report as *Members2* using **File-Save As.**

Customising a report

Changing the reports area

The area of each section of a report – the header, detail and footer sections – may be altered individually. Also the position of the right and bottom edges of a form may be adjusted.

To alter the depth of a section of the form, move the pointer to the bottom edge of the section, where it will change shape. Drag the pointer to a new location.

To alter the area of the report, drag the right and bottom edges to the size that you require.

Deleting, adding and restoring fields to and from a report

When you create a report from scratch it is necessary to add appropriate fields from a selected table or query. You may also wish to add or delete fields when changing an existing report. Again, the procedures are similar to those for deleting, adding and restoring fields to or from a form.

Changing the text of a field name label

The text of a field name label may be edited and, if required, additional text can be added to the form. Again, the procedures are similar to those for forms.

Task 4: Creating a customised report

We wish to open the report that we created earlier, **Classes**, and to add fields and modify field labels as indicated below, in order to create a report like the one shown below:

Chelmer Leisure and Recreation Centre. Sports, Fitness and Exercise Classes

Classes

Number:		1	Class Tutor:	Evans
Class Day:	Monday		Class Activity:	Ladies' Aerobics
Class Time:		10:00	Male/Female/Mixed:	Female

Number:		2	Class Tutor:	Franks
Class Day:	Monday		Class Activity:	Weight Training
Class Time:		11:00	Male/Female/Mixed:	Male

1   First open the report called **Classes** by selecting the report in the Database Window, and then selecting the **Design** button.

2   Now add the fields to the report by displaying the Field List window, by clicking on the **Field List** button or by using **View-Field List**.

3   Select all fields by clicking on the Field List window title bar.

4   Drag one of the fields to where you want the fields to start in the Detail band. Field names will be added to the left of the fields.

5   Click on the fields and their labels and move them into a more satisfactory position. Rearrange them as necessary.
    You may wish to use **Format-Align-Left** to align a group of controls (select them as a group first).

6   When all fields are added satisfactorily, close the Field List window, by, for example, double-clicking on its control box.

7   Edit the field label **Class No** so that it reads **Number**, by selecting the field label control, clicking where the text editing is required and modifying the field name label. Modify other labels as necessary in the same way.

8   Press *Enter* or click on another part of the report to complete the changes.

9   Try aligning groups of controls to achieve a tidy looking form.

10 Next, create a report header and a report footer by choosing **View-Report Header/Footer** so that a tick is placed beside this option.

Next create a control box into which you can insert the text, thus:

11 With the toolbox displayed, click on the Label tool (see FIGURE 21.1). Place the pointer in the **Report Header** box and drag it to create a box large enough to accommodate text.

12 Type the following text into the report header band: ***Chelmer Leisure and Recreation Centre – Sports, Fitness and Exercise Classes***.

13 Repeat these steps to insert text in the report footer, page header and page footer bands.

14 Print Preview the report, save it as ***Classes*** and close it.

You have now created a basic report showing all of the basic information, but clearly there is much scope for improvement in its format. A few of the possibilities are explored in the last tasks in this unit, but the majority are the subject of the next few units.

Reformatting a report

Altering the size and font of controls

To alter the size of the font of the controls on a report:

1 Select the controls to be altered.

2 Click on the **Font list** box in the toolbar and select the font required.

3 Click on the **Font Size** list box and select the point size required.

 If you increase the size of a font you may need to alter the size of the control and the size of the section.

Adding headers and footers

Page headers and footers can easily be added to a report. With the toolbox displayed click on the Label tool. Place the pointer in the appropriate header or footer box and drag it to make a box large enough to accommodate the text.

Task 5: Reformatting a report

This task reformats the report created in the previous task using a number of additional features that have been introduced above.

1   Open the report called **Classes** in Design mode.

2   Select the controls in the Report Header, open the Font Size list box and select an appropriate larger point size. Click on the **Bold** button to make the text bold. Click on the **Centre** button to centre the text within the control. If necessary, stretch the control box to display all of the text.

3   Move the field labels into the page header band by first selecting them as a group. Choose **Edit-Cut** and click anywhere in the page header, then choose **Edit-Paste**.

4   Rearrange the labels in the page header to make column headings. Select these as a group and format them by making them bold and italic and of a slightly larger point size.

5   Adjust the size of the page header so that it just accommodates the labels by dragging the bottom of the page header.

6   In the Detail band, rearrange the controls to align with the labels in the Page Header. If necessary, expand the boxes to accommodate the longest field value. For example, make sure that the control box for **Activity** accommodates Badminton.

7   In turn select the text boxes for **Class No** and **Time** and left justify them by clicking on the **Align Left** button. Select the Male/Female/Mixed control box and delete it by pressing the *Delete* key.

8   Select and format the report footer in bold and italics

9   Note that it will probably be necessary to move back and forth between Print Preview and Design mode a few times as you make changes and would like to view the results of those changes.

10 Print Preview, save as **Classes2**, close and print as required.

Chelmer Leisure and Recreation Centre.
Sports, Fitness and Exercise Classes

Number:	Day:	Time	Activity	Tutor:
1	Monday	10:00	Ladies' Aerobics	Evans
2	Monday	11:00	Weight Training	Franks
3	Monday	15:00	Body Conditioning	Latham
4	Monday	19:00	Step Aerobics	Wheildon
5	Tuesday	10:00	Men's Multi-gym	Jackson
6	Tuesday	14:00	Ladies' Multi-gym	Adams
7	Tuesday	19:00	Family Multi-gym	Jackson

Note: Tools

The report design window has a number of tools that you have been benefiting from in designing a report. It is useful to review these briefly.

1 The Ruler measures the distance from the top and left corners of the report. The Ruler can be removed or replaced by choosing **View-Ruler**.

2 The Grid is an organised layout of dots. Access automatically aligns moved or sized controls with the grid. The Grid can be moved or replaced by choosing **View-Grid**. To deactivate the Grid choose **Format-Snap to Grid**.

3 The Align option: use **Format-Align** to position controls relative to each other. Select controls, then choose **Format-Align** and the appropriate alignment, e.g. left.

Integrative tasks

Use the following tasks to practise the report creation skills you have gained from this and the previous three units.

Task 6: Creating a single-column report using Report Wizard

You require a report, based on the **Membership** table, which lists the following details for all members who are smokers:

- Membership No
- Category No
- Title
- Firstname
- Lastname
- Occupation
- Date of Birth
- Sex.

1 First define a query that allows you to select the records for the members who are smokers.

2 Save this query and then use it in the design of a report using Report Wizard.

Don't forget to save the report, as ***Smokers***, and print preview it on screen before seeking to print it.

Task 7: Creating a groups/totals report using Report Wizard

You wish to create a report that lists all of the classes offered by the centre, based on the **Classes** table. The report is to be organised in groups according to Class Activity. All fields in the **Classes** table are to be included in the report.

1   Produce a second groups/totals report, based on the **Classes** table, which details all of the information in the **Classes** table.

2   Sort the report in classes order.

3   Save this report as *Classes List*.

Task 8: Creating a customised report

Instead of using Report Wizard to create the report in Task 6, attempt to create the same report independently of the Report Wizard tool, i.e. as a customised report.

Types of form controls

What you will learn in this unit

This unit describes the additional features that you can add to forms and reports. At the end of this unit you should be able to:

- identify the tools in the Toolbox

- understand the functions of the different types of control.

So far you have met forms and reports created by AutoForm, AutoReport, and the Wizards, which tend to use limited controls. In this unit we will introduce the range of controls that can be added to both forms and reports. The level of sophistication that can be given to controls adds to the professionalism of the database application that is being created.

Types of form controls

In creating forms and reports you will have met labels and text box controls. If you are familiar with Windows applications you will be aware that there are other types of control, which you will have met when using dialog boxes. These include list boxes, check boxes and option buttons.

There are three categories of control.

1 *Bound controls*. A bound control is associated with a field in the table or query that was used to create the form. We have met text boxes, which are the most common type of bound control. Through a bound control, data can be displayed or altered.

2 *Unbound controls*. An unbound control is independent of the data in the form's table or query. Labels used as titles are examples of unbound controls.

3 *Calculated controls*. A calculated control is an expression. Usually the expression performs a calculation upon data in the form's table or query.

The Toolbox

The Access Toolbox allows you to add control objects to forms and reports. The Toolbox only appears while you are in design mode. If it is not visible in design mode then use **View-Toolbox** to make it visible. The Toolbox is composed of a set of buttons, and by clicking on a button that particular tool becomes available. Each button gives access to a different tool; the icon on the button indicates the function of the tool, as outlined in FIGURE 21.1.

Pointer		Control Wizard
Label		Text box
Option Group		Toggle button
Option button		Check box
Combo box		List box
Command button		Image
Unbound object		Bound object
Page break		Subform/Subreport
Line		Rectangle

FIGURE 21.1

Tool	Function
Pointer	This is the default tool when the Toolbox is displayed. Click on this tool to deselect a previously selected tool and return the mouse pointer to its normal function.
Label	Allows you to draw a rectangle (frame) on the form into which text can be inserted.
Option Group	Creates a frame of adjustable size into which controls can be placed. Only one of the controls within the frame can be selected. Usually the controls are of the same kind, e.g. option buttons or check boxes. When a control within an option group is selected, all others in the group are deselected.
Option button	Creates a round button that switches between on and off when clicked with the mouse. Option buttons are most commonly used within option groups to select between values in a set.
Combo box	Creates a combination box, which is a combination of a text box and a drop-down list box. This allows the choice of either selecting from a list or keying in an entry.
Command button	Creates a command button. A macro can be assigned to the button which will execute when the button is clicked.
Unbound object	Adds an OLE object, that is something created by another application which supports OLE, for example, a Microsoft Excel spreadsheet.
Page break	Causes the printer to start a new page at the location of the page break on the form or the report.

Tool	Function
Line	Creates a straight line that can be sized and relocated. The colour and width of the line can be changed using the properties and palette.
Control Wizard	When this button is depressed it enables the Control Wizard, so that if, say, the button tool is selected then the button wizard comes into operation. If the wizards are not required, then make sure that this button is not depressed.
Text box	Creates a frame in which text is displayed or edited. This is the most common form of control.
Toggle button	Creates a button that switches between on and off when clicked with the mouse
Check box	Creates a check box that toggles on and off. Multiple check boxes can be used in groups, but not within an option group, so that more than one check box can be selected.
List box	Creates a drop-down list box from which an item or value can be selected.
Image	Creates a frame for displaying a static picture on a form or report. Once added to a form or report the picture cannot be edited. Useful for a company logo.
Bound object	Where the data table contains OLE objects, for example, digitised photographs in a personnel table, this tool is used to create an object control in a similar way to the text box control.
Subform/Subreport	Adds a subform or subreport to a main form or report. Do not use this unless the subform or subreport already exist. See Unit 33 for more details about subforms and subreports.
Rectangle	Creates a rectangle which can be sized and relocated. Select width, colour and fill from the properties and palette.

Adding controls to forms

What you will learn in this unit

Controls on forms can be made more versatile by the use of list boxes, option buttons, option groups etc, features encountered in dialog boxes. If the entry for a control can be selected from a list – for example, rooms in a leisure centre – then data entry can be made more efficient by providing a list box. The person entering the data simply selects from the list rather than having to key in the entry. This has the advantages of reducing error and maintaining consistency.

Calculated controls may be added to either forms or reports. They display information that can be calculated from existing data. The example that is used in this session is that of calculating which members have not renewed their membership. At the end of this unit you should be able to create:

- a calculated text box

- a list box

- an option group

- a combo box

- a check box.

Adding controls to forms

This activity uses the Toolbox to add controls to forms. If the Toolbox is not visible in form design mode choose **View-Toolbox** to display it. Move it by dragging its title bar to a suitable place on your screen. As the best way to see how to add controls is by experimentation, this activity is comprised entirely of tasks. By completing these tasks you should acquire the skills with which to attempt a form design of your own.

Task 1: Creating a calculated text box

In this task the calculated control that is to be created is one that flags members whose renewal is due. This control will be added to the **Membership** form created in Task 1 in Unit 14. Before continuing, it will probably be necessary to review and amend the dates of joining and the dates of renewal to make this task realistic.

When people join Chelmer Leisure and Recreation Centre they pay for membership for one year from that date. They renew their membership annually. To calculate whether the member's subscription is overdue, the renewal date is compared with today's date. If the renewal date is before today's date then the fee is overdue. To create a realistic number, say three members overdue, amend or add records to the **Membership** table with appropriate dates for renewal.

1 Open the **Membership** table using the **Open** button to display the data.

2 View each record in turn and look at the **Date of Last Renewal** field.

3 Make amendments, if necessary, to the **Date of Last Renewal** fields so that some members have a date of renewal before exactly one year ago from today and others after that date.

To add the calculated text box:

1 Open the **Membership** form in Design view.

2 Click on the Text Box tool in the Toolbox.

3 Click on a suitable place on the form for the text box and its label.

4 Edit the label to read ***Subscription:***.

5 Click in the text box and key in the expression: ***=iif(DateAdd ("d",365,[Date of last renewal]) <Date(),"Overdue","Up to date")***.

If you miss out a bracket, when you press *Enter* Access will display an information box. Click on **OK** and you will be returned to the control so that you can edit the expression.

If you have trouble seeing this expression you can display it in a zoom box by clicking on the Control Source property and pressing *Shift+F2* to open the zoom box for editing.

6 Edit the name in the Text Box property window to read ***Subscription.***

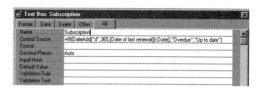

7 Run the form.

If you have errors return to the design view and check that you have keyed in the expression correctly. For example if you have misspelt the control name, then the message #Name? appears in the control. Check all control names carefully and correct them.

> **Subscription:** #Name?

Note: if you rename a control in an underlying table then this kind of error may result and the names in the expression will need to be amended accordingly.

The expression is an in-line IF....THEN.....ELSE statement. DateAdd adds one year to the date of the last renewal. This is compared to today's date. IF the result is less than today's date THEN the subscription is overdue ELSE it is up to date.

8 Save the form.

If you wish to create your own expressions refer to the Access Answer Wizard in the Help menu for lists of functions available.

Formatting displayed values

Font and size formatting are discussed in Units 14, 15 and 26. Typefont (bold, italics, underlining) and alignment (left, centre, right) can be chosen from the toolbar. Formatting can also be applied to the controls introduced in this session.

Task 2: Adding a list box

List boxes are useful for picking values from a static list of options that you create. You may define a list or use a table as a source of the list. The example that will be considered is that of adding a list box to the bookings form. The list box will be defined for the **Room/Hall/Court** field and will use a static list. This static list is a list of rooms at the leisure centre. At Chelmer Leisure and Recreation Centre there are six bookable rooms, the Fitness Suite, Sports Halls 1 and 2, and three courts.

1 To add a list box to the **Bookings** form, first open the form in Design mode.

2 Select and delete the **Room/Hall/Court** text box.

3 Open the Field List Window and choose **Room/Hall/Court**.

4 Check that the **Control Wizard** button in the Toolbox is depressed and click on the List Box tool.

5   Click and drag the **Room/Hall/Court** field from the Field List to the former position of the **Room/Hall/Court** text box. Adjust the controls on the form so that there is room to have a list box approximately deep enough to show all six rooms. If the list box is made smaller it will be shown with a vertical scroll bar. You may wish to try a slightly different layout as illustrated later in this task.

6   Click on the List Box tool in the Toolbox.

7   Click and drag the **Room/Hall/Court** field from the Field List window to the former position of the **Room/Hall/Court** text box.

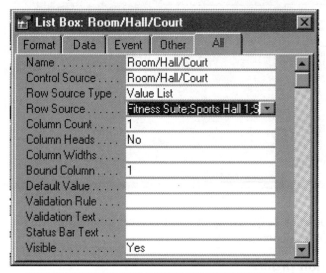

8   The **List Box Wizard** dialog box displays (provided the █ **Control Wizard** █ button in the toolbox is depressed). Select the option 'I will type in the values that I want' and click on █ Next> █.

9   Enter 1 into the Number of columns box. Click in the first cell and type **FITNESS SUITE**. Complete the column with **SPORTS HALL 1**, **SPORTS HALL 2**, **COURT 1**, **COURT 2** and **COURT 3** so there are six rows in column 1. Click on █ Next> █.

10 Choose the option 'Store that value in the field' and click on █ Next> █.

11 Accept the label for the list box, which should be Room/Hall/Court, and click on █ **Finish** █.

12 Click on the **Form View** button on the toolbar to display the form.

If adjustments to the position of controls are needed then return to the design mode to make them. The form could look something like this:

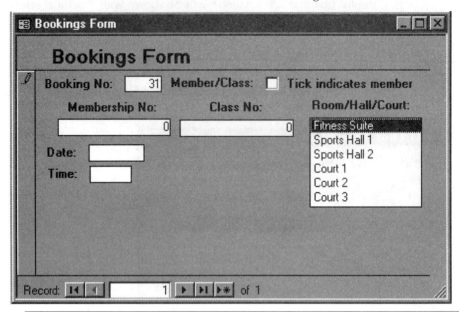

13 Save the form as **Bookings 2**. Try using the form to enter a booking. You may wish to amend the Tab Order depending upon your design.

Task 3: Adding option groups

Option buttons are commonly employed in Windows applications to select one option from a set of choices. They are best used where the value of the option is numeric, for example the categories of membership. To illustrate this an option group will be added to the **Membership** form. Open the form in design mode. Adjust the area of the form to allow room for the option group at the bottom or side of the form.

To create an option group:

1 Click on the Option Group frame tool in the Toolbox.

Check that the **Control Wizard** button in the Toolbox is depressed.

2 Choose **Category No** from the Field List and drag to the form.

Dragging is important because it links the control with the field. Release at a suitable position.

3   Enter the label names as shown in the illustration and click on Next> .

4   Select the option 'No, I don't want a default' and click on Next> .

5   The default values are correct so click on Next> .

6   Choose the option 'Store the value in this field: Category No' and click on Next>
    .

7   Choose the Option buttons type of control with an Etched style and click on
    Next> .

8   Give the option group the title ***Category No*** and click on Finish .

9   To test the form click on the Form View button.
    The already existing Category No text box control should serve to confirm the
    entry in the option group. Data could be entered into this field using either of the
    controls. Experiment by entering a new member's record.

10 Save the form as ***Membership***.

Task 4: Adding a combo box

In this task a combo box will be added to the **Membership** form for the choice of
county. Three counties will be listed but the text box will accept an alternative,
which may be keyed in.

1   Open the **Membership** form in design view.

2   Select and delete the County text box.

3   Check that both the Field List window and the Toolbox are displayed. Check that
    the Control Control Wizard in the Toolbox is depressed.

147

4 Click on the Combo Box tool in the Toolbox. Click and drag the **County** field from the field list onto its former location on the form.

5 Using the Wizard, opt to type in the values. Set the number of columns to one.

6 Enter the list of counties: **_Cheshire, Staffs, Derbyshire_**.

7 Choose the 'Store the value in this field: County' option and edit the label if required. Click on **Finish** .

8 Click on the **Form View** button on the toolbar to display the form. The County text box should have a **List Box** button, which when clicked will display the list of counties.

Notice that when entering a new record Cheshire is still the default county. If adjustments are needed, return to design mode. When complete save the form. Experiment with entering data.

Task 5: Check box controls for logical fields

In this task the Sex and Smoker controls in the **Membership** form will be changed to check box controls.

1 Display both the Toolbox and the Field List.

2 Delete the **Smoker** field.

3 Select the Check Box tool in the Toolbox. Click on the **Smoker** field in the Field List and drag onto the form.

4 Repeat for the **Sex** field.

5 Save the form.

Using filters to select records

What you will learn in this unit

Filters are used in conjunction with tables, queries and forms as a means of displaying selected records. A filter will 'filter out' only those records that match specified criteria and only display these records. When a filter is created it is stored with the table, query or form and can quickly allow users to view their data using the filter criteria without having to resort to creating a query. Trends in data may be identified using this method of data filtering. Information concerning, for example, poor membership in a certain category, or room usage can easily be obtained. Only one filter is stored with the table, query or report but it may be changed if necessary. If you make changes to a filter and do not want to save them then when you close the table, query or form say 'No' to the save changes question.

In this unit you will see how to:

■ use a filter to select records using one field as a criterion (Filter by Selection)

■ use a filter to select records using more than one field as criteria (Filter by Form).

A common business need is to select out a particular set of data, e.g. a list of customers of a particular type, say, small businesses. A datasheet or form displays all of the records in its underlying table or query; by attaching a filter selected records only will be displayed. Using the buttons on the toolbar, the filter can easily be switched on or off.

As we have already seen, queries can display a selected set of data. The advantage that a filter offers is that it can be designed while viewing the form, table or query. If records are being amended then it can be useful to select certain records, for example, to change a room for a particular activity.

Filter by selection

A filter created by this method will select records that match the value of the field selected. To filter by this method:

1 Select a field displaying a value which is your criterion, e.g. Meirton in the **Town** field. Click on the **Filter By Selection** button in the toolbar. The filter control buttons are shown below:

 Filter By Selection

 Remove Filter

2 Only the records with that value in the field will be displayed. To sort the records displayed via the filter use the sorting buttons on the toolbar as described in Unit 6.

3 To remove the filter click on the **Remove Filter** button.

Task 1: Selecting with a filter

In this task the **Membership** form will be filtered to display only those records where the **Town** field is Meirton.

1 Open the **Membership** form in Form view.

2 Move through the records until you find one for Meirton.

3 Click in this field and click on the **Filter By Selection** button.

4 Move through the records to view only the Meirton ones.

5 Click on the **Remove Filter** to display all the records.

6 Close the form.

Filter by form

A filter created by this method will select records that match the value of more than one field. Alternatives may be included, for example, Meirton and Branford in the **Town** field.

 Filter by Form

To filter by this method:

1 Click on the **Filter by Form** button in the toolbar. This displays a filter form, the one illustrated in FIGURE 23.1 is for the **Membership** form.

FIGURE 23.1

2 Using the filter form, specify the criteria for record selection. When you select a field you can open a drop-down list which displays all of the different values used for that field in the underlying data.

3 You may specify AND criteria by setting values in one or more fields, say all men in category 1.

4 You may specify OR criteria using the 'Or' tab. This will display another sheet of the form filter. The rules of AND and OR logic apply to sheets of the form filter in the same way as rows in the query QBE grid.

5 Click on the **Apply Filter** button on the toolbar.

6 To remove the filter click on the **Remove Filter** button.

Task 2: Selecting with a filter form

This task will use the **Membership** form and apply a filter to it. Open the **Membership** form in Form View. The filter buttons should be in the toolbar. To select records using a filter form:

1 Click on the **Filter by Form** button and the filter form window appears.

2 In the **Town** field select Branford. Click on the 'Or' tab and select Meirton.

3 Click on the **Apply Filter** button to see the selected records displayed in the **Membership** form.

4 To order the records by Category No select the category number field and click on the **Sort Ascending** or **Sort Descending** button.

Editing a filter

If you create a filter using Filter by Selection this filter will be saved with the form. To change it to use a different field value for selection purposes, simply select that field value and click on the **Filter By Selection** button. If you wish to filter by form instead then click on the **Filter by Form** button and specify your criteria in the form.

The same procedure is used to edit a filter that was created using the filter by form technique.

Task 3: Editing a filter

This task follows on from Task 2.

1 Click on the **Filter By Form** button to re-display the form filter.

2 Remove the town criteria by deleting them. Set criteria in the **Category No** field to filter out categories 3 or 4.

3   Click on the **Apply Filter** button to see the records.

4   Experiment with different filter forms, selecting using criteria for different fields.

5   Remove the filter and close the form.

Using controls in reports

What you will learn in this unit

In reports ordering is achieved by using the Sorting and Grouping button on the toolbar. Sorting and Grouping enhances the presentation of data in reports. The addition of a group header and footer identifies the group within the report. The field that is being used for grouping usually has its control in the group header acting as a heading. Calculated controls can be added to group footers to produce sub-totals or averages for the group. Records may be displayed in different orders within groups; for example, members may be listed alphabetically by last name within category grouping, bookings may be listed in time and date order within room grouping.

At the end of this unit, you will be able to:

■ save a form as a report

■ add controls to reports

■ add calculated controls to grouped reports.

Saving a form as a report

If you change a form to a report then you have more control over the variety of ways in which the data can be formatted for printing. For example, you can create a **Group/Totals** report from the data. To save a form as a report:

1 From the form design choose **View-Toolbars**.

2 Click on Customize in the **Toolbars** dialog box. In the **Customize Toolbars** dialog box, click on Form & Report Design in the Categories box.

3 Drag the **Save As Report** button to the toolbar, and click on **Close** . Note: you will not need to repeat these three steps next time you want to save a form as a report.

4 Click the **Save As Report** button on the toolbar. A dialog box appears with the name of the form as the default name. Either accept the name or type in a name for the report, and click on **OK** .

5 Close the form and click on the **Reports** tab in the Database window

6 Select the report and preview it. Make any adjustments to the design before printing. Note that if the Keep Together property of the detail section is set to Yes, then page breaks will not occur in the middle of records.

Task 1: Saving a form as a report

In this task the **Bookings** form will be saved as a report.

1	Open the **Bookings** form in design view.	If there isn't a **Save As Report** button on the toolbar, then follow steps 1 to 3 outlined above.
2	Click on the **Save As Report** button.	A dialog box appears with Bookings as the default name. Accept this.
3	Close your form and click on the **Reports** tab in the Database window.	
4	Select the **Bookings** report and preview it.	
5	Use Sorting and Grouping to group by room and to sort in date and time order.	Refer to Unit 18 if you need a reminder about how to do this.
6	Make any adjustments to the design before printing.	

Adding controls to reports

Calculated controls

Calculated controls are useful in reports. If a report has been produced from a table that contains data about stock in the form of quantity sold and price, then the sales revenue can be calculated by multiplying the quantity sold by the price. Another example is a logical field where instead of printing Yes or No you wish to print Male or Female.

Task 2: Adding a calculated control to the Members2 report

Use the report **Members2** customised in Unit 20. The aim is to add the fields **Sex** and **Smoker** but in such a way that Male or Female and Smoker or Non-Smoker are printed.

1	Display the report in Design mode.	
2	Rearrange the controls as illustrated below, making space to insert the calculated controls.	

3 Click on the Text Box tool and click in a suitable location for the information about sex.

4 Edit the label to read **Sex:**.

5 Key the expression **=IIF([Sex],"Male","Female")** into the text box.

   IIF is short for IF...THEN...ELSE, i.e. IF the field **Sex** is true THEN print Male ELSE print Female.

6 Click on the Text Box tool and click in a suitable place for the information about whether the member is a smoker or not.

7 Delete the label part of this control.

8 Key the expression **=IIF([Smoker],"Smoker","Non-Smoker")** into the text box.

   IF the field **Smoker** is true THEN print Smoker ELSE print Non-Smoker.

9 Save the report, preview and print it.

Membership No:		1	Category No:		2
Forenames:	Andrew J		Surname:	Walker	
Occupation:	Builder		Date of Birth:	12/3/52	
Sex:	Male		Smoker		

Controls in grouped reports

The most usual way of grouping records is by category. An example that was used in Unit 18 was that of the categories of membership. To group by category the best way is to choose to group by a particular category when constructing the report using the Report Wizard.

To alter the grouping properties once into design mode of the report use the **Sorting and Grouping** dialog box. This dialog box can be used to add group headers and footers. Calculated controls can be added so that, for example, group sub-totals or averages can be added to the report.

Task 3: Adding calculated controls to a grouped report

1   Display the **Membership2** report in design mode.

2   Click on the `Sorting And Grouping` button in the toolbar and set the sorting and grouping as illustrated below.

This report sorts the members into alphabetical order within the category number groups. For Category No set the Group Header and Group Footer to Yes, and set Keep Together to With first detail, which will prevent a page break between the group heading and a following detail.

3   Move the control for the **Category No** to the Category No group header. Select the control, use **Edit-Cut**, click on the Category No header bar and use **Edit-Paste**.

4   In the Category No group footer add a text box control and key into it the expression *=Count([Membership No])*, which will display the total number of members in each category.

5   Add a label reading: *Number of Members*.

6 Add a line at the bottom of the Category No footer.

| Page Header |
| Category No Header |

Category No: | Category No

Detail

Membership No:	Membership No
Forenames:	Forenames		**Surname:**	Surname
Occupation:	Occupation		**Date of Birth:**	Date of Birt
Sex:	=IIf([Sex],"Male","Fe	=IIf([Smoker],"Smok
Sporting Interests:	Sporting Interests

Category No Footer

Number of Members: =Count([Membershi|

Page Footer

=*Page*

7 Preview the report, save and print it. A selected part of the printout is shown below:

Membership No:		10	
Forenames:	George W F	**Surname:**	Weiner
Occupation:	Electrician	**Date of Birth:**	10/2/58
Sex:	Male	Non-Smoker	
Sporting Interests:	Weight training, squash		
		Number of Members:	7

Task 4: Groups within groups in a report

Continue from the previous task. The aim is create a report which groups by town within each category group. Display the report in design view and display the **Sorting and Grouping** dialog box.

1 In the fourth row add the field **Town**. Select this row and drag it to below the first row.

Priority of grouping can be changed by rearranging the rows in the **Sorting and Grouping** dialog box.

2 Select Yes for Group Header and Group Footer.

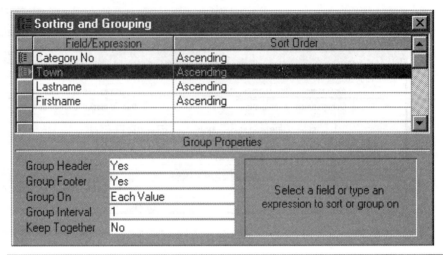

3 In report design mode move the control for **Town** to the Town Group Header.

4 Copy the calculated control for number of members from the Category No group footer and paste the copy into the Town group footer. Amend the labels for both these controls so that you know which is which.

5 Preview the report, save and print it.

6 Experiment with different sortings and groupings.

Controls design: integrative tasks

The following tasks revise some of the topics covered in this and the previous two units.

Task 5: Adding a combo box to the classes form

In this task a combo box will be added to the Classes form for the choice of tutor. Six tutors will be listed but the text box will accept an alternative, which may be keyed in.

1 Open the **Classes** form in Design view.

2 Select and delete the Tutor text box.

3 Check that both the Field List window and the Toolbox are displayed.

4 If the **Properties** dialog box is not shown click on the **Properties** button.

5   Check that the **Control Wizard** button is depressed in the Toolbox. Click on the **Combo Box** tool in the Toolbox. Click and drag the **Tutor** field from the field list onto its former location on the form.

6   Using the Wizard, opt to type in the values and set the number of columns to one.

7   Enter the list of tutors:
- Adams
- Evans
- Franks
- Jackson
- Latham
- Wheildon

8   Choose the Store in Class Tutor field option and edit the label if required. Click on **Finish**.

9   Click on the **Form View** button on the toolbar to display the form. The Tutor text box should have a **List Box** button, which when clicked will display the list of tutors' last names. If adjustments are needed return to design mode. When complete save the form. Experiment with entering data.

If you complete the **Tutor** table (compose the records yourself) then the tutors' last names are held in this table. This table could be used as the source for the combo box. This has the advantage that as tutors leave or new ones are employed the list in the combo box reflects the tutors' last names in the **Tutor** table. To make this change:

1 After dragging the **Tutor** field to the form, choose 'I want the combo box to look up the values in a table or query'.

2 Select the table **Tutors** and select **Lastname** from the available fields list.

3 Adjust the width of the column and continue with the wizard as usual.

Task 6: Adding a calculated control to a report

Use the **Classes2** report created in Unit 20 and group it by Tutor.

1   Move the **Tutor** control to the Tutor group header.

2   Add a calculated control in the Tutor group footer which will *count* the number of classes.
    Hint: count the **Class No** field.

3   Within the Tutor grouping try to group by activity and count the number of classes of each activity held by each tutor.

Adding lines and rectangles

What you will learn in this unit

This unit is the first of a series that focus on features that allow you to adjust the appearance of the information on a report or form, and to make their presentation more exciting. Access offers a wide range of tools for formatting both screens and reports, and supports the imaginative creation of interesting screens and reports. While all of these features can be applied to both forms and reports, some features are used more often with forms and others more often with reports. At the end of this session you will be able to:

■ add lines and boxes to forms and reports.

Understanding design

These units focus on those tools that are concerned with screen and report design. You will already have used some of these features briefly in the last few units. Forms and reports created using Wizards use some of these features to a limited extent, but by the time you have completed these units you should be able to improve on Wizard designs.

Although the tools we explore in these units allow you to be very adventurous with your designs, remember that good design hinges on the appropriate and sparing use of objects such as boxes and lines, and upon the use of only a limited number of different fonts. In addition, most organisations will wish to establish a house style which might be applied to all screens and groups of similar reports. We are not this consistent in the forms and reports that we generate in these units, because the range of forms and reports used here have been used to demonstrate the wide range of features and designs that can be adopted. When, however, you do need to create a house style, form and report templates are one means of doing this and we introduce these briefly in later units. The tips below act as a reminder of good design features.

Design tips: forms

1 Keep the form simple and easy to read. Don't use unnecessary text and graphics, but do use fonts and font sizes that are easy to read on the screen.

2 Use colour sparingly, to make forms interesting, but choose colours that are comfortable for those working at the screen for a long period of time.

3 Design the form taking into account how it will be used, i.e. where data needs to be entered and ease of movement between data entry boxes.

4 Maintain a consistent appearance for related forms. This looks more professional and makes it easier for a user to acclimatise to a series of forms.

Design tips: reports

1 Keep the report simple. Make the data easy to read by choosing font sizes and types that print well. Use fonts and graphics to help to convey important messages in the report.

2 Design in the knowledge of the capabilities of the printer. In particular, colour printers can produce much more intricate detail than non-colour printers.

3 Consider the application of the report. Who are the readers and why will they be using the report?

Adding lines and rectangles to forms and reports

Lines and rectangles can be added to reports and forms to emphasise portions of the form or report or to separate one part of the form or report from another.

Lines are added thus:

1 Select the Line tool in the toolbox.

2 Point to where you want the line to start.

3 Drag the pointer. The Line tool draws a line from where you start dragging the pointer to where you release the mouse.

Rectangles are added thus:

1 Select the Rectangle tool in the toolbox.

2 Point to where you want one of the corners of the rectangle.

3 Drag the pointer to where you want the opposite corner to be.

Changing control layers

When you add boxes to a form or report, they are initially placed on top of any other controls, and will, for example, cover text boxes so that their details are concealed.

In order to display controls that have been covered, you can take one control and put it behind another. For example, you may move controls hidden by a rectangle so that they are on top of the rectangle.

1 To move a control from the front to below other controls, select it and choose **Format-Send to Back**.

2 To move a control from behind other controls and put it on top, choose **Format-Bring to Front**.

Task 1: Adding lines and rectangles

Open the form **Classes**. Experiment with adding lines and rectangles to the form as suggested above, until it looks similar to the form shown below.

More specifically:

1   Move and size the controls so that they are in the position shown in the illustration.

2   Edit the text of the labels appropriately.

3   Place a box around the text in the form header.

4   Select the box by clicking on it and practise deleting it by pressing the *Delete* key. You are likely to need to delete lines or boxes that you have placed in the wrong place before you have finished!

5   In order to view the text you will need, with the box selected, to choose **Format-Send to Back**.

6   Place a box around the controls in the Detail band. Again, use **Format-Send to Back** to display the text.

7   Insert a line underneath the controls for Day and Time.

8   Save the form as Classes3.

Style enhancements

What you will learn in this unit

Style enhancements include alignment, colour, three-dimensionality, fonts and borders. These properties are listed in the bottom half of the Property Sheet window and may also be set using buttons on the toolbar. When a control is selected that uses any of the style enhancements described in these units, the middle and right section of the toolbar change to show the buttons in the table listed below. At the end of this unit you will be able to:

■ use different alignments

■ use different fonts

■ set dimensions

■ set colours

■ set borders.

Setting alignment and font

This activity explores the use of the toolbar to set alignment and font. To set alignment or font, first select the control to which you wish to add style and then click on an appropriate icon on the toolbar as required:

Alignment

left aligns text

centres text

right aligns text

Font

MS Sans Serif ▼   font name , which sets the style of characters

8 ▼   font size , which sets the size of the characters

B   **bold** , which sets characters as bold.

I   **italics** , which sets characters as italic

U   **underline** , which sets characters as underlined

Alignment determines whether the characters that appear in the control start at the left side of the control, end at the right side of the control or are centred in the control's position. The default alignment is right alignment for data fields containing numbers and dates and left alignment for all other controls.

It is useful to examine the alignment of controls during the design phase. To do this, select the control by clicking on it, and then examine which of the alignment buttons is depressed. The best alignment depends on how the controls have been arranged on the form or report. For example, in a report showing data in columns with field labels in the Page Header, set the alignment of the headers to the same as that for the entries below them in order to align the headings with the data.

A font is a collection of features that describes how the text appears. Using two or three different fonts, and using a larger font size, bold or italics can emphasise parts of a report, and make your form or report more interesting.

Note: although it is possible to set every control to a different font, good design requires that you be selective in the use of a range of fonts. In particular, you might consider the following.

■ Do not use more than two or three fonts on one report or form.

■ Select a font that is appropriate for the application For example, script and other fancy fonts are not often used in business applications and, where they are used, they are used deliberately for effect.

■ It is usual to use screen fonts for screen display and printer fonts for printing. If you use, for example, a screen font for printing a report, Windows makes the closest possible substitution and there will be a difference between what you see on the screen and what is printed on paper. If you have TrueType fonts, use them. They appear the same printed and on the screen.

■ Access remembers the printer that is currently selected when you create a form or report and uses fonts specific to the selected printer.

Task 1: Setting alignment and fonts on forms

Open the form **Classes3** used in Unit 25. Set the alignment of the text of the labels, and the font of the text of the labels as shown below:

More specifically:

1   Make the font size of Class No, Day and Time larger.

You may also need to increase the size of the controls in order to accommodate the text of the labels and the data in the larger size.

2   Click on each control in turn and check its alignment.

Left align controls for all fields except **Class No**, which should be right aligned.

Task 2: Borders, lines, alignment and fonts on reports

In this task you are required to apply borders, lines, alignment and fonts to a report, rather than to a form.

Open a new report, **Classes4**, based on the **Classes** report created earlier. Format the report so that it looks like this:

Chelmer Leisure and Recreation Centre.

List of Classes

Classes

Class No:	1

Day: Monday **Time:** 10:00

Tutor: Evans **Activity:** Ladies' Aerobics

Female

Class No:	2

Day: Monday **Time:** 11:00

Tutor: Franks **Activity:** Weight Training

Male

Class No:	3

View the report on screen and save it as **Classes4**. More specifically:

1   In the Report Header insert two controls and type in the text shown in the illustration. Move the controls to centre them. Centre align the text in the controls. Format the text to an appropriately large size and bold. Insert a box around the text. Use **Format-Send to Back** to re-display the text.

2   In the Detail band, first add the controls using the Field List. Click on the **Field List** window title bar to select all fields, and then drag one of the fields to where you want the fields to start within the Detail band.
Fields and their field names will be added to the Detail band.

3   Edit the field names so that they match those shown in the illustration.

4   Move the controls to match the arrangement in the illustration.

5   Format the text in the controls to a slightly larger size and size the controls appropriately.

6   To align a group of controls select the group and apply **Format-Align-Left/Right**. Most of these controls are left aligned with respect to each other.

7   Next examine the alignment of text within the controls. Ensure that all controls are left aligned, and, in particular, remember to left align Time.

8   Insert a box around the **Class No** controls. Insert a further box to enclose all text in the Detail band.

9   In the Page Header band type in *Classes*. Format this text and place a line underneath it.

10 At the top of the page footer band insert a line.

11 Examine the report in Print Preview, noting especially that no text is truncated by controls that are too small.

12 Make any necessary adjustments, Print Preview again, and save the report as *Classes4*.

Special effects, colours and borders

What you will learn in this unit

You can make a control look three-dimensional, add colour or set borders to different widths, to make reports and forms look more exciting. Remember that since most reports are not printed in colour, colours are most likely to be useful for on-screen forms and do not normally need to be set for reports. Equally, three-dimensional controls are particularly useful on forms, where they may be used to highlight labels or to mark out a button. At the end of this unit you will be able to:

- set dimensions
- set colours
- set borders.

Using the Formatting (Form/Report Design) toolbar

Special effects, colours and borders can be set using the Formatting (Form/Report Design) toolbar.

An alternative way to set these properties is through the Property Sheet window. This can be displayed by double-clicking on the control or area whose properties are to be viewed and changed. Generally, it is easier to use the formatting toolbar, so we shall restrict ourselves to its use here.

Each drop-down button allows the control of Back Color , Fore Color , Border Color , Border Width and Special Effects .

Back, fore and border colours

A control can have separate colours for back(ground), fore(ground) and border. To set a colour:

1 Select the control

2 In turn, click on the drop-down arrows of the Back Color , Fore Color and Border Color buttons to drop down the colour selection box, and choose an appropriate colour.

3 If the [Transparent] button in the colour selection box is clicked, the selected control becomes transparent so that the control shows whatever controls are behind it.

 Experiment with different colours until you have chosen a colour combination that is legible and that draws attention to appropriate parts of the screen.

Border widths

All controls have adjustable borders. Some controls, such as the labels for check boxes, option buttons and text boxes, as a default do not display any border. Other controls, such as option groups, list boxes and combo boxes, as a default display a thin black border.

To select a border width click on the drop-down arrow of the [Border Width] button on the toolbar. From the selection shown choose an appropriate border width.

Special effects

Special effects can be set as one of the following types: Flat, Raised, Sunken, Etched, Shadowed and Chiselled. Normal is the default for most controls. These options are displayed by clicking on the drop-down arrow of the [Special Effects] button on the toolbar.

Notes

1 When you select Raised, Sunken, Etched, Shadowed or Chiselled, the control adopts the same colours as buttons on the toolbar and command buttons to achieve the effect. These colours are set by the Control Panel program. It is only possible to change the fore and back colours.

2 When a control is shown as Raised, Sunken, Etched, Shadowed or Chiselled changing the border width will cause the control to revert to Flat.

Task 1: Setting dimensions and borders

Open the form **Classes3** and experiment with setting dimensions, colours and borders. For example, try:

1 Setting all of the field labels as Raised.

2 Setting the Form Header as sunken.

3 Selecting the line in the Detail band and making it wider.

4 Applying some colours to different parts of the screen to make it look interesting.

Control default properties

What you will learn in this unit

In earlier units we have set the properties of controls after we have added them to the form. It is also possible to set defaults for controls, which then apply to all of the controls of that type that you add to the current form or report. If you want to use a set of default control properties for multiple forms or reports, you can create templates that store default settings, and then use these templates whenever you create forms and reports. Templates will be explored in the next unit. At the end of this unit you will be able to:

■ examine the default properties of a control

■ set default properties of a control.

 While it is useful to note that it is possible to modify the default settings for a number of different types of controls, we do not recommend that you attempt this until you are sure that you understand which settings you are changing. There is immense potential for getting into an irretrievable muddle once you start to modify default settings. Proceed with caution!

Setting property defaults

To set property defaults for a form or report you follow similar steps to those for property setting:

1 Click the tool in the toolbox, while the Property Sheet window is displayed. Use **View-Properties** to display the Property Sheet.

2 The Property Sheet window changes to show only the properties that you can set as the default for controls of the selected type, e.g. text, date or number.

3 The title bar changes to Default and the name of the object. Most of the properties listed you should recognise from earlier activities, when you were setting the properties of the individual controls.

4 Change the properties in the Property Sheet window as you would change the properties for specific parts of forms or reports.

5 Any control of that type that you subsequently add to the form or report uses the new settings you have made for the control.

FIGURE 28.1 shows the **Default Properties** box for a section in a form, showing the Special Effect property drop-down list box.

FIGURE 28.1

Default text box

Clicking on the **Text Box** button in the Toolbox will display the default Text Box window.

Most of the property settings in the Property Sheet window will be familiar, but there are five new properties which are specific to default control setting:

Property	Description
Auto Label	Causes labels to appear with, for example, text boxes
Add Colon	Causes colons to appear at the end of labels
Label X and Label Y	Set the relative distance from the upper left-hand corner of the selected control
Label Align	Sets the position of the text in the label

Task 1: Examining the default properties of a control

To minimise the danger of you modifying the default settings in ways in which you did not intend and thereby finding it difficult to follow later activities in this book, this task concentrates on examining the existing default settings rather than modifying them. Note that adjustments to default settings will apply thereafter until they are again changed.

1   Open any form or report.

2   Select a section control by clicking on it. Click on the label button in the Toolbox. Open the Property Sheet window. Examine the default properties for this tool.

3   In a similar way, examine the Property Sheet window for a text box control.

4   Again, similarly, examine the Property Sheet window for a box or a line.

What are some of the differences between the defaults that are set for these different types of controls?

Report and form templates

What you will learn in this unit

When a form or report is created without using a Wizard, Access uses a template to define the default characteristics of the form or report. A template for producing reports or forms can be used in order to maintain a house style in form or report design, or, more simply, to avoid having to format all sections of the form or report on each occasion. For example, you may choose to set a range of default settings for specific parts of a form. Alternatively, you may have an earlier version of a report design that you need to upgrade and from which two similar, but different, reports might be created. A report template can be created from the first report, and that template used as the basis for the design of the two subsequent reports.

At the end of this unit you will be able to:

- create a form template
- create a report template.

Understanding templates

A template determines the default settings for form, report, section and control properties, section sizes and whether the form or report includes headers and footers.

To create a template from an existing form or report:

1 Create a form or report on which the settings for controls are as you want them to be.

2 Display the form or report header and footer and page header and footer, if you want these to be included in the default.

3 Set section sizes to determine their default size, if you want these included.

4 Save this form or report.

5 To use the form or report as a template, choose Tools-Options and click on the Forms/Report tab.

6 Type in the name of the form or report in the Form Template or Report Template box. Click on OK .

When you next create a new blank report the selected report or form will be used as a template.

 The default form template and report template are called NORMAL.

Task 1: Creating and using a report template

In this task we use a report that you have previously created to define the properties of a template. The most obvious properties that will be set are the section sizes (e.g. the size of the Page Header) and the presence or absence of various headers and footers. Other section and control properties have also been set.

1 First create a report template by opening the report **Classes4**.

2 Display the report header and footer, and page header and footer, to include these in the default.

3 Save this report as *Classes4*.

4 Next, to use the report as a template, choose **Tools-Options** and click on the Forms/Reports tab.

5 After 'Report Template' in the bottom of the dialog box, enter the name of the report, *Classes4*.

6 Select **OK**, and this will be used as the default report template.

7 Now, create a new blank report (note: the report may be based on a table or query) without using the Wizard.

8 You should see that this report has the same headers and footers and section sizes as the template. Close the report without saving.

Task 2: Creating and using a form template

In this task we will create a blank form and define some of the properties of the form to be stored in the template. The properties that will be redefined are those of the label tool.

1 First create a form template by clicking on the **Forms** tab and choosing New and clicking on Design view without basing the form on a table or query.

2 Display the form header and footer, to include these in the default. Adjust the size of these if desired. Set the label default properties to Times New Roman, size 14, bold and shadowed (see Unit 28).

3 Save this form as *Chelmer*

4 Next, to use the form as a template, choose **Tools-Options** and click on the **Forms/Report** tab.

5   After 'Form Template' at the bottom of the dialog box, enter the name of the form, **Chelmer**.

6   Click on   OK , and this will be used as the form template.

7   Now, create a blank new form (note: the form may be based on a table or query) without using the Wizard.

8   Note that the form has the same headers and footers and section sizes as the template. Use the label tool and note that it has the properties as set in the template. Close this form without saving.

Task 3: Returning form and report templates to Normal

To return the form and report templates to normal:

1   Choose **Tools-Options** and click on the   **Forms/Reports**   tab.

2   In the Form Template text box, enter **Normal**; repeat for **Report Template**.

3   Click on   OK .

Report and form graphs

What you will learn in this unit

Analysis of the data in a database can often be effectively performed and subsequently displayed with the aid of a graph. For example, it might be useful to examine the membership of the leisure centre by Membership Category or to look at the distribution of bookings and to display this data as a graph.

Graphs can be created by using Microsoft Graph, which is a component of both Access and Word. Here we introduce a few tasks that make use of Graph in order to demonstrate how it can be used to insert graphs into a report or form. These tasks first take you step-by-step through the creation of a simple graph, and then demonstrate how that graph can be inserted into a report or form. If you require more detailed help on the use of Graph, consider using Help in Access or work through the relevant exercise in *Word 7 for Windows 95: A Progressive Course* by S.J. Coles and J.E. Rowley (DP Publications, 1996).

At the end of this unit you will be able to:

■ add a graph to a report or form

■ edit a graph

■ understand the links between the database and the graph

■ use the clipboard to copy or move graphs

■ add a graph to a report that is based upon a query.

Understanding graphs

Graphs are often most appropriate in reports where some summary data can be displayed pictorially. As such, they will often be included in the footer for a report.

Graphs can also be added to forms. We start to demonstrate the process by creating a graph in a simple form, which we could display on the screen as a quick summary that displays the prices for the various different membership categories. This is about the only sensible graph that we can create relating to the data in the **Chelmer** database that does not involve the use of a query. Later we experiment with some simple graphs that make use of queries to show counts of the occurrences of specific field values, for example to show the bookings by the room, hall or court that has been booked. We also experiment with moving graphs between forms using the clipboard.

Adding a graph to a form

Graphs can be used on forms to display data on screen at a glance. The simplest use of graphs is where the data comes from the tables, but the same data is shown on each screen. This is the type of graph that we shall explore here.

You may also create a graph that changes with each record. For example, a simple graph may show the inventory information for one product. When another product is displayed another graph will be displayed. In this case it is likely that basic information about the product, such as its name and supplier, may be called from one table, and data concerning inventory levels drawn from another table that stores order records. Such a graph involves the use of multiple tables.

To use a graph in a form to display summary data from a table:

1 Display or create a form in Design view. Insert a heading in the Form Header e.g. **Chelmer Leisure**.

2 Prepare to insert a graph in the Detail band by ensuring that it is open, by clicking on it.

3 Choose **Insert-Chart**. Drag a chart box onto the detail band area.

4 When you release the mouse button, Access presents a series of dialog boxes to help you define your graph.

5 Go through the dialog boxes, making appropriate selections for fields to chart and label the graph and inserting a graph title.

6 To complete the graph, choose the **Finish** button.

7 Access now inserts a control in the Detail band which accommodates the graph.

8 Save and close the form. The graph is saved as part of the form

Task 1: Adding a graph to a form

In this task we add a graph to the Detail band in a form.

1 First open a new form in Design view. Choose to use the table **Membership Category**.

2 Insert the following heading in the Form Header: *Look how competitive our membership rates are*.

3 Prepare to insert a graph in the Detail band by ensuring that it is open, by clicking on it.

4 Choose **Insert-Chart**. Drag a chart box onto the detail band area.

5 When you release the mouse button, Access presents a series of dialog boxes to help you define your graph.

6 Select a data source for your graph, i.e. the table **Membership Category**. Click on **Next>**.

7 Select **Category Type** and **Membership Fee** as the fields to be graphed. Click on **Next>**.

8   Select a graph type. Choose a column chart and click on Next> .

9   Click on the Preview Chart button to see a preview of the chart. Click on Close and then on Next> .

10 Give your graph a title, e.g. **Membership Fees**. Choose the option 'No, don't display a legend'. To complete the graph, click on Finish .

11 Access now inserts a control for the graph in the Detail band.

12 To see the graph on the form click on the Form View button.

You may need to adjust the size of the graph control in design view. The graph may need editing and this is discussed in the following section.

13 Save the form as **MemCatGraph** and close the form. The graph is saved as part of the form.

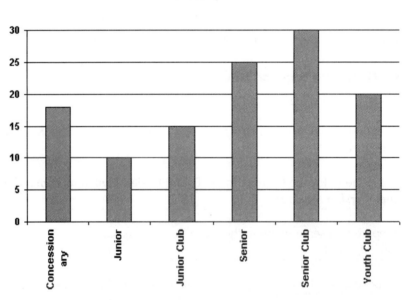

Editing a graph

Graphs can be edited in order to change the data that is displayed, or the way in which it is displayed. For example, in the graph in Task 1, the *y* axis numbers could be shown as £s. Graph is a powerful graph creation tool which allows you a wide range of different options for creating and designing effective graphs. In Task 2, we demonstrate how to use Graph to make a few simple alterations to a graph.

To edit a graph:

1 In Design view, double click on the graph.

2 Access starts Graph and displays the graph in the graph application window.

3 Make any changes that you require.

4 Choose **File-Exit & Return to FormName: Form.**

5 Save and close the form or report. The graph is saved as part of the form or report.

Task 2: Editing a graph

This task edits the form that you created in Task 1. We experiment with some basic editing techniques in order to demonstrate the principles. More specifically, we shall format the graph title and tick mark labels, and place a border around the graph.

 The commands may be slightly different on your computer, depending on which version of Graph you have.

1 Open the form **MemCatGraph** in Design view and double-click on the graph control to start Graph.

2 Choose a different type of chart, by clicking on the down arrow of the **Chart Type** button and selecting a bar type chart.

3 Add or remove the gridlines by clicking on the Horizontal or Vertical Gridline buttons in the toolbar or using **Insert-Gridlines.**

Further gridline formatting may be achieved by selecting a gridline and using **Format-Selected Gridlines.**

4 Insert an axis label for the horizontal axis (*y* axis), by choosing **Insert-Titles-Value(Y) Axis.** Click on **OK**.

This will give you a small area demarcated by boxes into which you can enter text.

5 Enter *Membership Price.* Next, click on this to display the text that you have entered. Double click on this label again to call the **Area Patterns** dialog box. Choose a larger font size and make the text bold and italic. Click on **OK**.

6 Click on the title to select it and press *Delete* to remove it.

7 Click on the vertical axis and choose **Format-Selected Axis.** Make the axis text larger and bold italic.

8 Click on the graph's data sheet, select the column of numbers, choose **Format-Number** and choose currency. Click on **OK**.

179

9   Choose **File-Exit & Return to MemCatGraph: Form.**

10 If necessary, size the control by selecting it and dragging its border in order to display the edited graph.

11 Save the form as ***MemCatGraph***. Close the form.

Demonstrating that graphs are linked to the database

The graphs that you create in Access and that use data in the database are updated when you update the data in the database. So, for example, the graph that we have just created should be automatically updated if we change the values in the Membership Category table.

Task 3: Testing links between the database and associated graphs

In this task we wish to demonstrate how the graph changes to display new data in the **Membership Category** table. Suppose that we change the fees:

1   Open the **Membership Category** table in datasheet view.

2   Edit the values in the **Membership Fee** column to:

Category No	Membership Fee
1	£30.00
2	£35.00
3	£15.00
4	£20.00
5	£23.00
6	£25.00

3   Close the **Membership Category** table.

4   Open the form **MemCatGraph** in Design mode. Examine the graph and check that it is displaying the new data.

5   Leave the form **MemCatGraph** open for the next task.

Using the clipboard to copy or move graphs

An easy way to insert a graph in a form or a report once you have created the report is to use the clipboard to cut or copy and paste the graph from one location to a second location.

Task 4: Using the clipboard to copy a graph

1   With the form MemCatGraph open in Design mode, as at the end of Task 3, click on the graph to select it.

2   Choose **Edit-Copy** to copy the graph to the clipboard.

3   Close the form MemCatGraph.

4   Create a new grouped report based on the **Bookings** table, using the Report Wizard. Include all fields.

5   Group by Room/Hall/Court and sort in Date order.
    Access automatically names and saves the report.

6   Open the new report in Design view. Click on the **Report Footer** bar and choose **Edit-Paste** to insert the graph into this report from the clipboard.
    The graph should now be inserted in the report.

Adding a graph to a report, with the aid of a query

The basic approach to creating a graph for a report is the same as that for creating a graph in a form. Task 4 demonstrated how to copy a graph into a report footer, but this is not a very useful chart to have in the report footer of a report that lists bookings. A more useful graph for such a report would display bookings according to some category, such as room, hall or court, or the category of membership. In order to create such a graph it is first necessary to create a query. Why?

If you think about the stages that you went through to create a graph in Task 1, you will remember that you needed to specify the two fields that were to be displayed on the graph. Suppose we wish to display the number of bookings for each room, hall or court. We need to display the values in the **Room/Hall/Court** field against the number of bookings for each of these. In order to do this we need a field called, say, **CountofBookings**. To create this field we need a query. Task 5 demonstrates how we might approach this.

Another interesting graph that we might add to a report that lists bookings is one that displays bookings by category type, i.e. how many bookings are made by each category of member. The creation of this graph would be more complex than the graph that we create below. Why? Because here we need to show **CountofBookings** by category type. This would involve creating a query that uses more than one table, and then basing the graph on that query. Which tables would you need to use in the query? Queries that use more than one table are introduced in Unit 32.

First, it is useful to record the steps for adding a graph to a report. To add a graph to a report footer:

1 Make 5 to 8 cm (2 to 3 inches) of space in the Report Footer section. Choose **Insert-Chart**.

2 In the grey area below the Report Footer section, draw a control that is about 5 cm (2 inches) deep and 15 cm (6 inches) wide.

3 When you release the mouse button, Access presents a series of dialog boxes to help you define your graph.

4 Go through the dialog boxes, making appropriate selections for fields to chart and label the graph, and inserting a graph title.

5 To complete the graph, choose the **Finish** button.

6 Access now inserts a control in the Report Footer for the graph and resizes the footer to make room for the new control.

7 To view the graph on the report, click on the **Print Preview** button and move to the last page of the report.

8 When you have finished looking at the graph choose **Close**.

9 Save and close the report. The graph is saved as part of the report.

The same principles apply for adding a graph to any other part of the report, such as the Report Header.

Task 5: Adding a graph to a report using a query

In this task we add a graph to the report footer in the report **Bookings**. First we need to create a query to use as the basis for the graph:

1 Create a new query using the **Bookings** table.

2 Add the fields **Booking No** and **Room/Hall/Court**.

3 Click on the ▐Totals▐ button to display the Total: row.

4 In the Total cell for the **Booking No** field insert *Count*

5 In the Total cell for the **Room/Hall/Court** field insert *Group By* and in the **Sort** row insert *Ascending*.

6 Display the dynaset and check that the query counts booking in categories as you would expect it to.

7 Save the query as *Bookings by Hall*.

Field:	Room/Hall/Court	Booking No	
Table:	Bookings	Bookings	
Total:	Group By	Count	
Sort:	Ascending		
Show:	☑	☑	
Criteria:			
or:			

Room/Hall/Court	CountOfBooking No
▶ Court 1	2
Court 2	1
Court 3	1
Fitness Suite	8
Sports Hall 1	1
Sports Hall 2	9

Now we want to use this query to create a graph:

8 Open the booking report created previously in Task 4 in Design view.

9 To remove the existing graph, click on it and press *Delete*.

10 Choose **Insert-Chart**. Drag a chart control in the Report Footer.

11 Access takes you through the creation of a graph using Graph Wizards.

12 Choose **Queries** and then **Bookings by Hall** as the data source for your graph. Add both fields to be displayed on the graph.

13 Choose a graph type, select column. Preview the chart.

14 In the **Linking Fields** dialog box choose <No Fields> for both fields.

15 Give your graph a title or accept the suggested title, i.e. **Bookings by Hall**

16 To complete the graph, choose the `Finish` button.

Access now inserts a control in the Report Footer for the graph and resizes the footer to make room for the new control.

17 To view the graph on the report, click on the `Print Preview` button and move to the last page of the report.

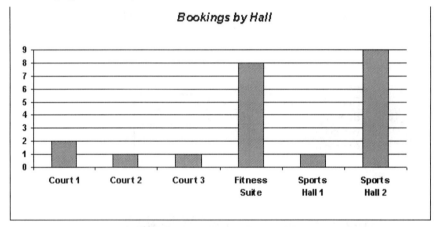

If you make the control too small to display a graph effectively, you cannot size the graph in Report Design view. You need to resize the control that contains the graph in Design view, and resize the graph in Graph.

18 When you have finished looking at the report in Print Preview choose `Close` to move back into Design view.

19 Double-click on the graph to take it into Graph and edit it as you choose.

The graph above has been sized so that the tick mark labels display effectively, and the title has been formatted. Choose **File-Exit & Return to Bookings by Hall: Report** when you have finished editing.

20 Save the report and close it.

The graph is saved as part of the report.

Forms and reports pictures

What you will learn in this unit

In the previous unit, we experimented with adding graphs to forms and reports. These are one type of object that can be added to forms and reports. You can also insert a picture from Windows 95 Paint, a worksheet object from Microsoft Excel, or any object from an application that supports object linking and embedding (OLE). At the end of this unit you will be able to:

■ add pictures and objects to forms.

■ add pictures and objects to reports.

Understanding pictures and objects

Here we briefly explore inserting a picture into a form or report. A picture can be created in Microsoft Draw (part of Microsoft Word), or with Windows Paintbrush. We use Microsoft Draw to create a picture and insert this picture into both a report and a form. If a field on a form, for instance, uses an OLE object data type, it is possible to display that object on the form. For example, in **Membership** we might have a field that accommodates a photograph of the member. This could be displayed on a form or printed on a report. Another application of a picture might be to insert a log into the Form Header on a form and the Report Header on a report. Since typically the same logo may be used on all forms and reports used by one organisation, in the tasks below we first create the logo for Chelmer Leisure and Recreation Centre, and then add it first to a form and then to a report.

Task 1: Adding a logo to a form

1 To create the logo using Microsoft Word, open WordArt by selecting **Insert-Object-Microsoft WordArt 2.0**.

2 Enter text for a logo and choose to make it slanting.

3 Embed this into the Word document.

4 Select and copy it.

5 Click on the **Create Picture** button on the Drawing toolbar and paste in the Word Art text. Add a border and a stickman drawing.

You may need to select **View-Toolbars** and click in the Drawing check box to display the Drawing toolbar.

6 Close the picture to embed it into the document.

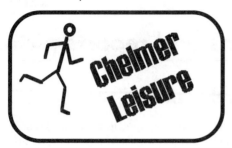

7 Copy it to the clipboard by selecting the drawing and using **Edit-Copy**.

8 Return to Access.

9 To add the logo to the form, open the form **Membership** in Design view.

10 Click on the Form Header section.

11 Choose **Edit-Paste**, size the Header section and position the logo.

12 Save the form and close it.

Integrative tasks

Task 2: Creating a graph for the categories report

The **Categories** report was created in Report Wizards as a Groups/Totals report. It shows members grouped in categories. It might be interesting to create a simple graph that counts the members in each category and displayed the number of members in each category. It would be even better if the category labels were not shown as Category No, but as Category Type, but this would involve the use of a query that used multiple tables, and these are not introduced until later units. To create this graph:

1 First create an appropriate query to count members by Category No.
   You will have created such a query earlier but probably did not save it.

2 Revisit Unit 13 to discover how to create a query showing **Category No** and **CountofLastname**.

3 Save this query as **CATEGORIES**.

4 To create a graph in the report **Categories**, open the report **Categories**.

5 Go through the steps necessary to create a graph in the Report Footer, choosing the query **Categories** as the data source.

6 Edit the graph as appropriate.

Task 3: Adding a logo to reports

To start to create some kind of house style for our reports, we would like to add the Chelmer Leisure logo to some of the reports generated form the **Membership** table. The easiest way to do this is to copy and paste the logo that we created in Task 1 to the clipboard, and then to paste the logo into the Report Header of the report.

1 Open the form **Membership**.

2 Click on the Chelmer Leisure logo to select it. Choose **Edit-Copy**.

3 Close the form.

4 Open the report **Members**. Click on the Report Header, and choose **Edit-Paste**. The logo should appear in the Report Header.

5 Repeat this operation for the other reports you have created.

Using multiple tables in a query

What you will learn in this unit

This unit introduces queries that use more than one table. Tables are linked by their relationships and through these links can act as if they were one large table. At the end of this unit you should be able to:

- add and delete tables from a query
- create queries using multiple tables.

 In Unit 8 you saw how to set up relationships between tables, yet these relationships have not yet been used. The intervening units have introduced tables, queries, forms and reports. In the interests of simplicity these are based on one table or a query generated from one table. This and the next few units explore the use of more than one table. Queries can use more than one table and these queries can produce forms or reports.

Through constructing queries using more than one table, you should appreciate how versatile a relational database is. By keeping data in a series of linked but separate tables the need to duplicate data is reduced and it is simpler to update data. To illustrate this point, if the **Membership** table contained a **Fee** field, if the fee changed then every record would need amending rather than just the records in the **Membership Category** table.

Multiple tables in a query

When you use more than one table in a query there should be links between the tables chosen for the query. This is a good opportunity to review the relationships between the tables in the Chelmer Leisure and Recreation Centre database. The **Membership** table is linked to the **Bookings** table through **Membership No**. The **Membership Category** table is linked to the **Membership** table through the **Category No**. The **Bookings** table is linked to the **Membership** table through the **Membership No**. The **Bookings** table is linked to the **Classes** table through the **Class No**. The **Tutor** table is linked to the **Classes** table through the **Lastname**.

If tables are added to a query and there is no relationship defined between them then Access will try to link them, which could be a time consuming and unproductive process.

Joins between tables

Before you can use joins between tables, you must know the contents of the fields of the tables and which fields are related by common values. Assigning identical names to fields in different tables that contain related data is a common practice. This has been adhered to in the Chelmer Leisure and Recreation Centre database; for example, **Membership No**, which is the link between the **Membership** and the **Bookings** tables. There is an exception, which is **Class Tutor** (**Classes** table) and **Lastname** (**Tutor** table), which could be remedied by using **Tutor No** as a field in both tables.

Knowing the contents of your tables will help when you need to add tables to a query, so that you add the tables containing the data you wish to access and also any additional tables that are necessary to create links between the tables. This is discussed in more detail at the beginning of each multiple table query used in this activity.

Joins are indicated in Access query designs by lines between field names of different tables, as illustrated in Task 1.

Access allows different types of joins between tables, but only one type, the most common, will be considered here. This type of join is called an *equi-join* and this has already been created when the relationships were defined. Equi-joins display all of the records in one table that have corresponding records in another table. This correspondence is determined by identical values in the fields that join the tables. In the case of the Chelmer Leisure and Recreation Centre database, all joins are based on a unique primary key field in one table and a field in the other table in a one-to-many relationship (see Unit 8).

Adding tables

When creating a query this is simply a matter of selecting more than one table from the Show Table dialog box. Tables are shown in the Query window with lines between them indicating the relationships. If you omit a table then choose **Query-Show Table** to display the Show Table dialog box again.

Deleting tables

This a simply a matter of clicking on the title bar of the particular table and pressing the *Delete* key. However, check that the table was not providing an indirect link between two tables and also make any amendments to the query.

Task 1: Adding tables to the query window

In this task, all of the tables in the Chelmer Leisure and Recreation Centre database are added to a query.

1 Starting at the Database window, click on the Query tab and click on New. Select Design View and click on OK.

---

2 From the Show Table dialog box, add all the tables.
These are **Membership**, **Membership Category**, **Bookings**, **Classes** and **Tutors**.

---

3 By rearranging the tables, your query window will appear as illustrated below. If there are no lines or some missing indicating the relationships, abandon the query and check the relationships using **Tools-Relationships**. Refer to Unit 8.

 A link may be displayed between **Lastname** in the **Membership** table and **Lastname** in the **Tutors** table. This illustrates that the significance of field names should be considered when designing a table. However, the link can be removed by clicking on it and pressing *Delete.*

4 Delete the **Tutors** and the **Membership Category** tables.

Consider why it is dangerous to delete the **Bookings** table.

5 Close the query without saving it.

Using multiple tables

This section comprises a series of tasks in which questions are asked of the database and queries containing multiple tables are devised in order to answer the question posed.

Task 2: Membership fees

Q. How much membership fee money has been collected in the last six months?

A. First decide which tables are needed. The data needed is the members who renewed their membership in the last six months, their membership category and the amount of the fee. This data can be found in the **Membership** table and the **Membership Category** table. Is there a link between these two tables? Yes: between **Category No** (primary key **Classes** table) and **Category No** (**Membership** table), so only these two tables will be required.

Before continuing you should review the dates of renewal in the **Membership** table and if necessary update them so that several members will be selected by this query

To create the query:

1 From the Database window click on the Query tab and click on New . Select Design View.

2 From the Show Table dialog box select the **Membership** table and the **Membership Category** table.

These two tables should be shown in the query window with a link between them.

3 Add the fields **Membership No** and **Membership Fee** to the query.

4 Create a calculated field that works out the length of time between the date of last renewal and today's date. In the first field cell enter the expression: ***Rejoin: DateDiff("d",[Date of last renewal],Date()).***

This calculates the number of days from the date of the last renewal to today.

5 Run this query to see the result.

6 Return to the query design. Add the criteria *<182* (you may need to check your records to see if this query will work) to find those with renewal dates less than six months old.

7 Run this query to check and then return to design mode.

8 Click on the Totals button to create totals.

9 In the **Rejoin** field select 'Where' in the total cell and hide this field. In the **Membership No** field select 'Count' and in the **Membership Fee** field select 'Sum'.

10 Run the query.

The result should be the numbers of members who rejoined in the last six months and the total of fees paid.

11 Save the query as ***RECENT FEES PAID***.

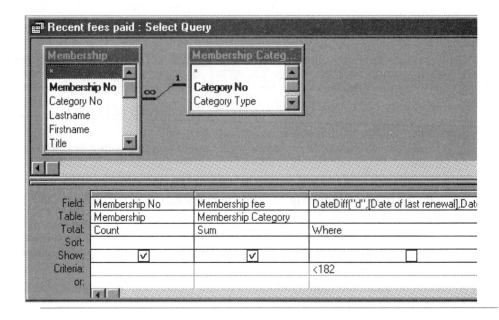

To create the report:

12 From the Database window click on the **Reports** tab and click on **New**.

13 In the **New Report** dialog box select the query 'Recent fees paid' from the drop-down list and use **AutoReport**: Tabular to design a report.

14 Switch to Design view and edit the labels so that your report is similar to the one below. Save the report as *Recent fees paid.*

Fees paid in the last six months

No of members joining	*Total fees paid*
8	£176.00

Task 3: Class activities in the fitness suite

Q. How can you find what class activities are being held in the fitness suite?

A. The tables that are needed to answer this question are the **Bookings** table and the **Classes** table. There is a direct link between these tables through **Class No**.

To create the query:

1 From the Database window click on the **Queries tab** and click on **New**. Select **Design View**.

2 From the **Show Table** dialog box select the **Classes** table and the **Bookings** table. These two tables should be shown in the query window with a link between them.

3 Add the fields **Member/Class**, **Room/Hall/Court**, **Class Day**, **Date**, **Class Time** and **Class Activity** to the query.

4 In the **Member/Class** column set the criterion to No to select only classes and hide this field.

5 In **Room/Hall/Court** put *Fitness Suite* in the criteria row and hide this field.

6 Run the query.

7 Save this query as *Activities in Fitness Suite*.

To create the report:

8 From the Database window click on the **Reports** tab and click on **New**.

9 In the **New Report** dialog box select the query **Activities in Fitness Suite** and use **AutoReport: Tabular** to design a report.

10 Edit your design to create a report similar to the one illustrated below. Save this report as *Activities in Fitness Suite*.

Class activities in Fitness suite

Day	Date	Time	Activity
Monday	13/5/96	10:00	Ladies' Aerobics
Monday	13/5/96	11:00	Weight Training
Tuesday	14/5/96	10:00	Men's Multi-gym
Tuesday	14/5/96	14:00	Ladies' Multi-gym
Tuesday	14/5/96	19:00	Family Multi-gym
Wednesday	15/5/96	10:00	Ladies' Aerobics
Thursday	16/5/96	15:00	Multi-gym
Friday	17/5/95	14:00	Men's Multi-gym

Task 4: Class attendance

Q. Which members are attending which classes?

A. Our database is unable to answer this question. Why? The data needed has not been recorded. The database could be modified so that this data can be added. What would be the best way to go about this? One method could be to introduce an extra field, **class**, which is added to the **Membership** table. However, this leads to problems if the member attends more than one class or if a class is cancelled. A better alternative is to create another table which keeps lists of members in classes. This table would be linked to both the **Membership** table and the **Classes** table. **Class List** would be a suitable name for this table.

To create the **Class List** table:

1 From the Database window click on the ▓Tables▓ tab and click on ▓New▓. Select Design View and click on ▓OK▓.

2 Create a table with two fields, **Class No** and **Membership No**. Make both fields numeric of type long integer.

This is so that they are of a type that will correspond to the counter types used by the fields **Membership No** (**Membership** table) and **Class No** (**Classes** table) to which they will be related.

3 Each record is unique; that is, the entire record not a field on its own. Therefore the primary key must be both fields. To set both as the primary key select both before clicking on the ▓Primary Key▓ button in the toolbar.

4 Define two relationships as described below.

In both of these relationships referential integrity is enforced. This will prevent a class or membership number being entered that does not exist in the **Classes** or **Membership** table, so a non-existent member cannot join a class nor can a member join a non-existent class.

5 Click on the ▓Relationships▓ button and then click on the ▓Shaw Table▓ button. Add the **Class List** table.

6 Drag **Class No** from the **Classes** table to **Class No** in the **Class List** table. Check the **Enforce Referential Integrity** box.

7 Drag **Membership No** from the **Membership** table to **Membership No** in the **Class List** table. Check the **Enforce Referential Integrity** box.

8 Save the layout and close the Relationships window.

Before a form can be created, a query linking the member's name to the class activity first needs to be created. A form can be created from this query which lists the names of members in each class (this form will later become a subform in a main/subform in Unit 33):

9 From the Database window click on the `Queries` tab and click on `New`. Select **Design View** and click on `OK`.

10 From the **Add Table** dialog box select the **Class List** table and the **Membership** table. These two tables should be shown in the query window with a link between them.

11 Add the following fields to the query: **Class No**, **Membership No**, **Firstname** and **Lastname**. Save the query as **Class Member List**. Close the query.

12 From the Database window click on the `Forms` tab and click on `New`. In the **New Form** dialog box select the **Class Member List** query just created and use AutoForm: Tabular to create a tabular form.

13 Display this form in design view and display the properties window. Click on each control in turn, except for **Membership No**, and set the Locked property to Yes and the Enabled property to No.

This prevents data being entered into these controls; as this form is intended to be a subform then you will see that it will not be necessary to enter data into these controls. Setting the Enabled property to No prevents the focus going to these controls.

14 Add a title to the form as illustrated and save the form as ***Class Member List***.

 15 See Unit 33 for the creation of the Main/Subform.

Main/subforms and main/subreports

What you will learn in this unit

Subforms and subreports are another way of making use of the links between tables. An example of this would be keeping academic information about students. A student may study several modules and for each one a performance record is kept. The details about the student – for example, Student No, Title, Surname, Forenames, Date of Birth, Date Enrolled, Personal Tutor – could be kept in a **Student** table. The module results for all students could be kept in a **Results** table, with fields **Student No**, **Module No**, **Coursework Grade**, **Exam Grade**, **Overall Grade**, **Date Completed Module**. The tables **Student** and **Results** would be linked through the **Student No**.

A link between the **Student** and **Results** tables enables a main/subform to be designed for entering module results. By designing a form based on the **Student** table and another form based on the **Results** table the two forms can be combined into one known as a main/subform. This form would display the student details as heading information and the results records for that student. A report can similarly be constructed. A **Student** report would be the main part of the main/subreport and a **Results** report would be the 'sub' part of the main/subreport.

At the end of this unit, you will be able to:

■ create and use main/subforms

■ create and use main/subreports.

Creating and using main/subform forms

What is a subform? A main form is usually created from one of the primary tables in the database and a subform is a table that is related to it. This is best described by means of an example. Consider a wholesaler's database, where there is a table of customer names, addresses, etc and a table of purchase transactions made by customers. A form showing the customer's details plus a list of transactions made by that customer can be created using a Main/Subform.

The **Customer** table creates the main part of the form and that customer's transactions comprise the subform part. This type of form is useful for all areas of transaction processing, such as sales made by salespeople, or bookings made by members of a leisure centre.

A main/subform is created by inserting one form into another as follows:

1 Create both the main form and the subform separately. Ideally these should be linked through an existing relationship. The main form should be created in single-column format and the subform in tabular format.

2 Open the main form in Design view.

3 Choose the **Window** menu to display the Database window (shortcut key *F11*). If necessary click on the Form tab to show the list of forms.

4 Click and drag the subform to the main form.

Task 1: Creating and using a main/subform

This task creates a main/subform for the **Class List** table. This form shows the class details and lists members enrolled in the class in the subform. This form can be used to book members into a particular class. Open the **Classes** form and use **File-Save As** to save the form as **Class Lists**, which is a copy of the **Classes** form that can be modified. Display this form in design view and set the Locked property for all of the controls to Yes. This is the reason for making a copy of the form. The original **Classes** form can be used to enter classes data but this new form cannot.

1 Choose **Window-Tile Vertically** to display the **Class Lists** form window (in Design view) and the Database window side by side.

2 Click on **Class Member List** (the subform created in Task 4 in Unit 32) and drag to the **Class Lists** form.

A subform box appears on the form. You may wish to reposition and resize this subform box.

3 Run the form and it should appear similar to the one illustrated below.

4 Save the form.

5 Try using the form to enter data. A class list can be created by entering the membership numbers of those members who are attending the class.

6 So that a report can be generated later, enter data for three class lists as follows:

Class No	Membership No
1	2
1	5
1	16
4	4
4	6
5	7
5	10
5	1

Creating and using main/subreport reports

Like forms, reports can include subreports. An example of such a report is one in which a customer's details are shown in the main report and purchases made by that customer in the subreport. To insert a subreport into a main report:

1 Create both the main report and the subreport separately as reports. Ideally these should be linked through an existing relationship.

2 Open the main report in design view. Use Sorting and Grouping to add a group footer, for example group by customer or group by company, depending upon the nature of the subreport.

3 Choose the **Window** menu to display the Database window (shortcut key *F11*). If necessary, click on the **Reports** tab to show the list of reports.

4 Click and drag the subreport to the required section in the main report.

Task 2: Adding a subreport to a report

For this task check that you have a **Classes2** report, which was created in Task 4 of Unit 20. Open it and save it as *Classes List2*.

In this task a report of classes and the members enrolled on each of the classes will be created. This is done by adding a **Class Member List** subreport to the **Classes List2** main report.

1 Save the form **Class Member List** as a report (see Unit 24) with the same name.

2 Open this new report in Design mode.

3 Reorder the fields so that **Class No** is last in the row. Set the Visible property for this field to No so that it does not print. Remove the label for **Class No**.

4 Edit the header to read *List of members*.

5 Use the palette to alter the colour of fill and borders. Preview the report to check your settings.

6 Save the report and close it.

7 Open the **Classes Lists2** report in design mode.

8 Click on the **Sorting and Grouping** button and select **Class No Ascending** in the dialog box. Set the Group header and footer to Yes.

9 If necessary, widen the group footer section to make room for the subreport.

10 Open the **Window** menu and choose Chelmer Leisure: Database to display the Database window.

11 Click and drag the **Class Member List** report into the group footer section.

You may need to rearrange your windows so that you can readjust the position of the subreport.

12 In the Subform/Subreport properties window note that the link between the two reports is **Class No**.

13 Set the Can Shrink and the Can Grow properties of the Class No Group footer section to Yes.

Click on the section header to select the section.

14 Delete the **Class Member List** label and adjust the size of the control as illustrated following. Preview the report.

15 The report would look better if the field labels were in the Class No Header. Cut and paste the headings from the Page Header to the Class No Header as illustrated.

16 Preview, make final adjustments so that it looks similar to the following extract and save the report as **Classes List2** before printing it.

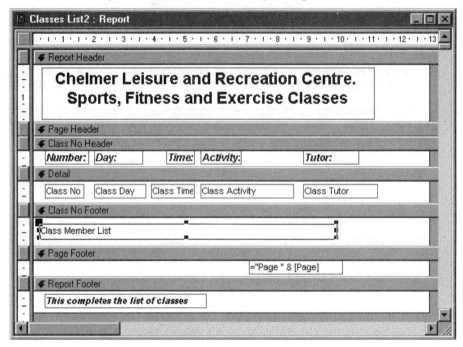

Action queries

What you will learn in this unit

Usually queries are passive in nature; that is, they do not change any of the data, they only retrieve it in response to criteria. However, special queries known as action queries can be designed to change the data. An example of this could be a bank amending its customer credit limits. The bank wishes to amend the credit limit of customers whose present limit is £200 or less and who have been with the bank for six months or more. First a query that selects the appropriate customer records would be constructed. By converting this search query to an action query the values in the **Credit Limit** field, for each selected record, would be updated with the new credit limit.

At the end of this unit, you will be able to:

■ design action queries to modify data.

Designing action queries to modify data

Previously we have used queries to interrogate the database tables. Action queries can be used in a more powerful way to amend the tables. There are four types of action query: update queries, delete queries, append queries and make table queries.

An action query changes the data in your table or copies data from one table to another. Unlike the select queries we have already seen, an action query does not show the records it has retrieved for modification.

If you wish to see the result of the change made by an action query then you will need to either convert your action query to a select query or open the table (if you have created, appended to or deleted from it) to view the changes. The following activities explore the various action queries.

Make table and delete query

These two action queries will be used together to deal with members who have not renewed their membership for more than a year. This operation would be carried out periodically, say annually or every six months, to keep only current members in the **Membership** table.

Members who have not renewed their membership could simply be discarded or their information could be kept in a separate file for a further time period as historical information. Chelmer Leisure and Recreation Centre follows the latter course and makes a table of old members before deleting them from the current membership table.

A make table query does just what it says: it creates one table from another or others. Data is selected by means of a query to create the new table. A delete query deletes a group of records from one or more tables. The query you design will select the records that are to be deleted. When you run the query, Access retrieves the records you asked for and deletes them from the table.

In this activity we will create a table in which to store old member details before deleting all of the members whose last renewal date was in 1994 or before. So that some records meet this criteria, open the **Membership** table and add a couple of records where the **Date of Last Renewal** is before the end of 1994.

Task 1: Archiving and removing out of date members

1   Start a new query using Design view. Add the **Membership** table to the query.

2   Add all the fields from the table to the query by double-clicking on the table's title bar and dragging the highlighted area to the field cell.

3   In the **Date of Last Renewal** column enter *<1/1/95* into the criteria cell.

You may wish to run the query to see which records are selected.

4   To create the **Last Renewed 94** table, use **Query-Make Table**, or click the **Query Type** button on the toolbar and select Make Table. Key in the name of the table *Last renewed 94*.

This table will go into the current database so do not change the option setting. Leave the check boxes at their default values.

5   Click on **OK**.

6   Click on the **Run** button. A message box confirms the number of records that are being added to the new table. Click **Yes** to create the new table.

7   Next change the query to a delete query by clicking the **Query Type** button and selecting Delete. Remove all fields except for the **Date of Last Renewal** so that the query is:

Field: Date of Last Renewal

Delete: Where

Criteria: <#01/01/95#

8   Click on the **Run** button. A message box confirms the number of records that will be deleted. Click Yes.

There is no need to save this query as it has performed its function.

9   View the tables to see the effect of the make table and delete actions.

Update query

An update query updates data in your tables. You choose the records and fields you want to update. When you run the query, Access retrieves the records you asked for (this is known as a dynaset) and makes the changes you specified. An example of an update query is increasing the credit limit of all customers who have credit limits of less than, say, £2000.

Task 2: Update query

An example of an update query that Chelmer Leisure and Recreation Centre might use is when a member of staff changes. The update query can change the name of the **Class Tutor** in the **Classes** table.

1   Start a new query using Design view.

2   Add the **Classes** table to the query.

3   Create a query with three fields: **Class No**, **Class Tutor** and **Class Activity**. In the criteria cell for Class Tutor put *"Franks"*.

4   Choose **Query-Update.**
    An Update To: row appears in the grid in the lower part of the query window.

5   In the **Update To:** cell of the **Class Tutor** column type *"Knight"*.
    An action query will change the data in your table.
    It is a good idea to check that your query will select the correct records before running the action query. You can do this by changing your action query into a select query.

6   First save the action query. Use **File-Save** and save it as *Update tutor*.

7   To change to a select query use **Query-Select**.

The lower grid changes to the select grid.

8   Click on the **Datasheet** button on the toolbar to view the query's datasheet.
    The data that you see is the data that will be affected by your action query.

9   To change back to the action query, first display the query design (click on the **Query Design** button in the toolbar) and choose **Query-Update**.

10 Click on the **Run** button on the toolbar. A message will appear telling you how many rows will be updated and giving you the opportunity to cancel. Click on **Yes** .

11 Close the query.

12 Create a search query using the new tutor's name as a criterion. Satisfy yourself that the action query has worked.

13 Delete the action query: in the Database window click on the query button, highlight the action query and delete it by pressing the *Delete* key.

Integrative tasks

The following tasks reinforce concepts introduced in this and the preceding units.

Task 3: Tutors' names and qualifications

Q. What are the names and qualifications of the tutors taking classes on 13/5/96?

A. The tables needed are the **Bookings** table and the **Tutors** table. There is not a direct link between these tables so the **Classes** table must also be included in the query. Before creating this query review the data in the **Tutors** table and create records for the tutors employed by the centre.

To create the query:

1 From the Database window click on the Queries tab and click on New. Choose Design view.

2 From the **Show Table** dialog box select the **Bookings**, **Tutors** and **Classes** tables. These three tables should be shown in the query window with links between them.

3 Add the fields **Date**, **Surname** and **Qualifications**.

4 In the **Date** column set the criterion to *#13/5/96#* and hide this field. Run the query.

5 Create a report based on this query.

Task 4: Finding non-smokers in the aerobics class

Q. How many members who attend ladies aerobics are non-smokers?

A. The tables needed are the **Membership** table, the **Class Lists** table and the **Classes** table.

To create the query:

1 From the Database window click on the Queries tab and click on New. Choose Design View.

2 From the **Show Table** dialog box select the **Membership**, **Class Lists** and **Classes** tables.
These three tables should be shown in the query window with links between them.

3   Add the fields **Lastname**, **Smoker** and **Class Activity**.

4   In the **Smoker** column set the criterion to No and hide this field.

5   In the Class Activity column set the criterion to *"Ladies Aerobics"* and hide this field.

6   Click on the **Totals** button and select Count for the **Lastname** field (only **CountofLastname** will show).

7   Run the query to discover the answer to the question.

8   Change the criterion for Smoker to find out the number of smokers attending ladies aerobics.

Task 5: Attendance profile

Q. What is the attendance profile of classes on Wednesdays?

A. The **Classes** and **Class Lists** tables are required for this query. However, before constructing it use the **Class Lists** form to enter members into Wednesday's classes. A report containing a chart is a good method of presenting the answer to the query.

1   Create a query as illustrated. Click on the **Totals** button to display the **Total** row. Hide the **Class Day** field.

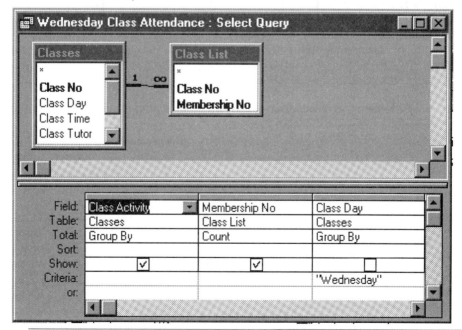

2 Save the query as *Wednesday Class Attendance*.

3 Create a columnar report based on this query using the Report Wizard. Add both fields, **Class Activity** and **CountofMembership No**, to the report and sort on **Class Activity**.

4 In the report footer create a chart, using Insert-Chart. Base the chart on the **Wednesday Class Attendance** query. Select both fields for the chart.

5 Accept the options offered by the Wizard but choose not to display the legend. Click on Finish .

The chart can only be seen in Report View; in Design View only the default chart is seen. Some editing of the default chart in terms of size and scale can be achieved to produce a result similar to that shown below. As results of editing changes cannot be seen until the report is viewed, patience and perseverance may be required.

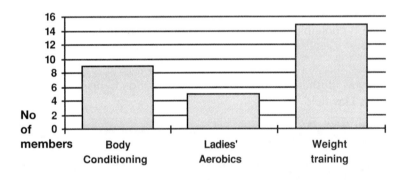

6 Save the report as *Wednesday Class Attendance*, and preview before printing.

Importing databases

What you will learn in this unit

This and the next few units explore various issues associated with the importing and exporting of data from other sources. At the end of this unit you will be able to:

- understand the distinction between importing data and linking data
- import data from databases created in Access 2 or earlier versions
- import data from other standard database packages such as dBase III, IV and 5, Microsoft FoxPro, Paradox and ODBC databases.

Understanding importing, exporting and linking files

Importing and exporting data is relatively straightforward with Access, especially between other standard packages and other packages in the Microsoft suite. Developers of the latest generation of database software have recognised that users now have significant databases established in earlier database packages and need to transfer data from these environments into any new database package that they acquire. Equally, users need to be able to integrate data in database, spreadsheet and word processing into appropriate documents. In general, no database or database product is standalone; it must interface effectively with other related products.

You should select and attempt those activities for which you have the appropriate software and data.

Access offers two different approaches to making use of existing data compiled with other database software.

1 Linked data behaves as if it is part of the Access database although it is not. The data can be edited in both Access and the other application and can be viewed as an Access table, although an Access table is not created. Linking is useful when you wish to maintain the data in its original file format, while creating Access forms and reports.

2 Imported data has been converted from its original format into an Access table. A copy of the data is placed in a table in an Access database.

Access supports linking and importing with dBase, FoxPro, Paradox and ODBC databases.

Other database objects, such as forms and reports, can be imported from another Access database. When importing, all or a subset of these objects can be chosen. In this way a database created in an earlier version of Access can be imported to Access 7.

If you want to add a table to an Access database, this data can be imported into an existing Access database.

If you want to add data from an existing application to an Access table, you can append the data to an Access table, as long as its format matches that of the existing table entries, i.e. it has the same fields with similar definitions.

Either link or import: do not do both, because this will create more than one copy of the data. With more than one copy of the data it is difficult to be sure which is the most recent and to maintain file integrity.

If importing an Access 2 (or earlier) database, create a new database using Access 7 first.

Exporting data puts Access data into a format that other applications can use. Exporting data creates a separate file that contains the data stored in a table.

Importing data into an Access table

To import the data in a file into a table in the current Access database:

1 Display the Database window.

2 Choose **File-Get External Data-Import** or click on the New Object button and choose New Table and Import Table.

3 Choose the format of the data to be imported from the 'Files of type' list box in the **Import** dialog box.

4 Select the drive from the 'Look in' list box

5 Select the directory and then the file you want to import and click on the **Import** button.

6 When Access has imported the file that you have selected, it displays a message to say that it has successfully imported the file. If Access needs some guidance on formatting the file as an Access table you will be prompted by a series of wizards.

7 Click on **OK** and close.

If the Database window is displaying the database's tables, the newly imported table should appear in the list of tables (FIGURE 35.1).

FIGURE 35.1

Importing Access database objects

You can import tables, queries, forms and reports from another Access database whether or not the database was created in a previous version of Access. To import Access database objects:

1 Display the Database window.

2 Choose **File-Get External Data-Import**.

3 Choose Microsoft Access from the 'Files of type' list box in the **Import** dialog box.

4 Select the drive from the 'Look in' list box

5 Select the directory and then the file you want to import and click on the **Import** button.

6 The **Import Objects** dialog box is displayed. Click the tab of the type of object you wish to import. Select one or more of the objects listed and click on **OK**.

7 The imported objects will be listed under the appropriate tab of the Database window (FIGURE 35.2).

FIGURE 35.2

The **Options** button provides choices such as importing a table structure without the data or importing queries as tables.

Linking a table

To link data stored in another file as a table in the current database:

1 Display the Database window.

2 Choose **File-Get External Data-Link Tables** or click on the **New Object** button and choose New Table and Link Table.

3 Choose the format of the data that you want to import from the Files of Type list box in the **Link** dialog box.

4 Select the drive, directory and filename of the file that you want to link and click on Link. There may be a further dialog box depending on the type of data you are linking, for example, links to index files used by dBase.

5 When Access has linked the file you have selected it displays a message saying that the attachment is complete.

6 Click on **OK** and close.

Linked tables are used in the same way as any other Access table. The link icon is displayed in the Database window, showing that there is a link to that table (FIGURE 35.3). Simply click on the table icon to use the table. Linked tables can be used with queries, forms and reports just like any other table.

FIGURE 35.3

To delete a linked table, if you no longer require the link:

1 Select the icon for the linked table that is to be detached.

2 Select **Edit-Delete**.

This deletes the link but the table remains intact, and could be re-linked at a later stage.

Differences between linking and importing

Imported and linked tables differ in the following respects:

1 They have different icons; compare FIGURES 35.1 and 35.3. Imported tables have the usual icon but are shown in upper case.

2 Deleting a table. When you delete an imported table, the table's contents are deleted. When you delete a linked table, the link is broken between the current database and the database that contains the table. The data is still available in the original database and any other databases that use the table as a linked table.

3 Adding data. Imported data can be added to an existing table or placed in a new table. Linked tables are separate from existing tables in the database.

4 Speed. Linked tables are not as fast as tables stored in Access files because the data from the linked table must be constantly read from the original file. Access to data in linked tables can be speeded up by appropriate use of queries and indexes.

5 Table design. Linked tables can only be modified to a limited extent in Table design. Features such as field names, data type, the order of fields, adding new fields or deleting fields cannot be performed on linked tables.

6 Importing or linking? If you link, the data remains in another database format and can still be used just as Access tables are used, for example, to edit data, and create queries, forms and reports that use data. If you intend to use your data only in Access you should import it. Access works faster with its own tables and Access tables can be customised more easily.

Task 1: Importing, exporting and linking files

This task asks you to review some of the basic concepts associated with importing, exporting and linking files. Answer the following questions:

1   What are the advantages of importing a file compared with linking it?

2   How can you tell when viewing filenames with the Database window which files are imported and which files are linked?

3   Why should you not both link and import a file?

4   What does exporting do?

Using dBase data with Access

dBase III, IV and 5 files can be imported or linked using the steps outlined above. There are only two special points to note:

1 In an imported table dBase field types are changed thus:

Character	⇨	Text
Numeric	⇨	Number
Float	⇨	Number
Logical	⇨	Yes/No
Date	⇨	Date/Time
Memo	⇨	Memo

In a linked table, the table continues with the original dBase field types.

2 In linking a dBase table the speed with which Access operates with the data in the dBase file can be improved by selecting appropriate dBase index files.

Task 2: Importing and linking dBase data into Access

In this task you first import, and then link, an existing dBase file into Access.

First, you require a dBase file to import. Either create a file in dBase, or use an existing dBase file. You could create a file such as:

Field	Field Name	Type	Width	Dec	Index
1	**AGENCYNO**	Numeric	3		Y
2	**SURNAME**	Character	20		Y
3	**INITIALS**	Character	3		N
4	**TITLE**	Character	10		N
5	**STREET**	Character	30		N
6	**TOWN**	Character	20		Y
7	**COUNTY**	Character	20		N
8	**POSTCODE**	Character	10		N
9	**DATEBIRTH**	Date	8		Y
10	**SEX**	Logical	1		N
11	**MARRIED**	Logical	1		N
12	**QUALIFICAT**	Memo	10		N

This could be a dBase file held by an employment agency called **AGENCY.DBF**. Make a copy of this file so that you have two copies. You are going to use one of these copies to import and the other to link.

Import the first copy thus:

1 Display the Database window.

2 Choose **File-Get External Data-Import**.

3 Choose the format of the data to be imported from the 'Files of type' list box in the **Import** dialog box.   i.e. select dBase III, IV or 5 (***.dbf**).

4 Choose the drive, the directory and the .DBF file that you wish to import and click on the **Import** button.   When Access has imported the file that you have selected, it displays a message saying that it has successfully imported the file.

5 Click on **OK** and close.   You will now see **AGENCY** listed with the other tables in the database.

6 Open this table and set **AGENCYNO** as the Primary Key. Set the index for **SURNAME** to Yes (Duplicates OK). Set the index for **TOWN** to Yes (Duplicates OK). Set the index for **DATEBIRTH** to Yes (Duplicates OK). Format **DATEBIRTH** to Short Date. Yes/No fields result in –1 for true and 0 for false. Set format for **SEX** to ;"Male";"Female" and that for **MARRIED** to ;"Married";"Single".

If the Database window is displaying the database's tables, the newly imported table should appear in the list of tables (it will be shown in upper case). Click on the table name and in Design view examine the table and observe that the field types have been changed to be consistent with Access field types.

Use the second copy of the file to link. Link this table by following these steps:

7 Display the Database window.

8 Choose **File-Get External Data-Link Tables**.

9 Choose the format of the data that you want to import from the Files of Type list box in the **Link** dialog box.

i.e. select dBase III, IV or 5 and click on **OK**.

10 Select the drive, directory and filename of the file that you want to link and click on **Link** .

11 Select the dBase index files (.NDX or .MDX). Choose Select. Click on **OK**.

When Access has linked the file it displays a message saying that the link is complete.

12 Click on **OK** and close.

If the Database window is displaying the database's tables, the newly linked table should appear in the list of tables. It will be indicated by a linked table icon.

13 Try to modify the linked and imported tables.

 Note that in Table Design an imported table can be modified in exactly the same way as any other Access table. The linked table can only be modified to a limited extent. You will find that you cannot change the structure, but the following properties can be set: format, decimal places, caption, default value, validation rule and validation text. Try changing some of these.

Complete the task by deleting the link to the linked table:

14 Select the icon for the linked table that is to be unlinked.

15 Select **Edit-Delete**.

Importing text/spreadsheets

What you will learn in this unit

It is possible to import spreadsheet data and text files into Access. Access can import files in the following spreadsheet and text formats:

- Excel (versions 2.x, 3.0, 4.0, 5.0 and 7)
- Lotus 1-2-3 or 1-2-3/W (**.WKS**, **.WK1** and **.WK3** files)
- Delimited text (where text is separated into groups by commas, tabs or other characters)
- Fixed width text (where values are arranged so that each field has a certain width)

At the end of this unit you will be able to:

- import spreadsheet data into an Access database.
- import delimited text files into Access.

Importing spreadsheet data

When a spreadsheet or text file is imported, Access creates a new table to store the imported data.

There are a number of options to be selected in importing spreadsheet data and text files into Access, because it is necessary to define how the table should be created from the spreadsheet data or text file.

Before attempting to import spreadsheet data into Access it is easiest if the data is in an appropriate format. The data must have the same type of data in each field and the same fields in every row. In addition, it is preferable if column headings of an appropriate type are inserted in the first row of the spreadsheet so that these can be used as field names. Access will look at the first row of data and assign a data type for each field on the basis of this first row. For example, if the first value for a field is a date, then Access assigns Date/Time data type to that field and assumes that all values for that field will be dates.

To import spreadsheet data into Access:

1 Display the Database window.

2 Choose **File-Get External Data-Import**.

3 Select the appropriate format for the data that you want to import (e.g. Excel) and the drive and directory that contains the file to be imported.

4 Select the name of the spreadsheet that you want to import and click on the ▇Import▇ button. Access will display an **Import Spreadsheet Wizard** dialog box (FIGURE 36.1).

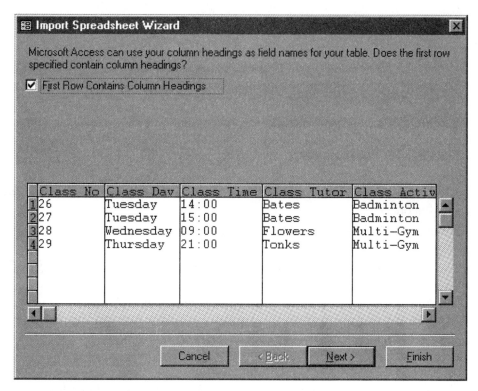

FIGURE 36.1

5 Tick the First Row Contains Column Headings check box if the spreadsheet range you are importing has labels in the first row that you want to use as the field names in the table.

6 Work through the Wizard's dialog boxes; to set indexes for the fields being imported; to set a primary key; and finally to name the table. Click on **Finish**.

7 When Access has imported the table, click on **OK**. The new table should be displayed in the list of tables in the Database Window.

Task 1: Importing spreadsheet data

Note: to complete this task you need access to a copy of Excel, Lotus or other compatible spreadsheet package.

Create a spreadsheet in Excel or Lotus 1-2-3 into which you can enter data that matches the **Classes** table. Save this file as *Classes2*. As illustrated below, enter the field names in the first row, and then enter some records for specific classes, one record per row, as required.

	A	B	C	D	E	F
1	Class No	Class Day	Class Time	Class Tutor	Class Activity	Male/Female/Mixed
2	26	Tuesday	14:00	Bates	Badminton	Female
3	27	Tuesday	15:00	Bates	Badminton	Female
4	28	Wednesday	09:00	Flowers	Multi-Gym	Mixed
5	29	Thursday	21:00	Tonks	Multi-Gym	Male

Open Access and open the Database window.

1   Display the Database window.

2   Choose **File-Get External Data-Import**.

3   In the 'Files of type' list box in the **Import** dialog box choose the appropriate format for the data that you want to import (e.g. Excel) and the drive and directory that contain the file to be imported.

4   Select the name of the spreadsheet that you want to import. Choose the **Import** button.
    Access displays the **Import Spreadsheet Wizard** dialog box.

5   Tick the 'First Row Contains Column Headings' check box. Click on **Next**.

6   The next dialog box allows you to specify information about each of the fields that you are importing. By clicking on each field in turn you can set field name, indexed (or not) and whether the field is to be imported. Use the default settings (i.e. don't make any changes) and click on **Next**.

7   You are prompted to choose the primary key for the new table. Choose **Class No** and click on **Next**. Enter the table's name, e.g. *Classes2*, and click on **Finish**. When Access has finished importing the table it will display a message to that effect.

8   Click on **OK**.
    The new table should be displayed in the list of tables in the Database window.

 If you choose to allow Access to analyse your table it will, when you ask, run the Table Analyzer Wizard, and inform you of the faults in your table design. Try this if you are interested. What is wrong with the design of this table?

Importing delimited text files into Access

A delimited text file is a text file in which fields are separated by a special character, such as a comma or a tab. Data in a text file intended for importing into a table must be in an appropriate format. As with spreadsheets, the text file must have the same type of data in each field and the same fields in every row. Again, the first row may be used as field names, and Access uses the first row of data as a basis for assigning data types. Note that only delimited text files, saved as **.txt** files, can be imported. So, for example, if you create a file in Word, you must save it as a **.txt** file and not a **.doc** file if you wish to import it into Access.

To import a delimited text file:

1 Open the Database window.

2   Choose **File-Get External Data-Import**.

3   Choose the appropriate format for the data you want to import (i.e. text files) and the drive and directory that contain the file to be imported.

4   Select the text file to be imported and then choose the `Import` button. The Text Import Wizard dialog box will be displayed.

5   Choose delimited as the format. Click on `Next`.

6   Specify the Text Delimiter that has been used, e.g. comma or tab. Click on `Next`.

7   Specify whether you would like to store your data in an existing table or a new table.

8   Specify the following information about each of the fields that you are importing: field name, data type, whether indexed and whether the field should be included. Click on `Next`.

9   Choose the Primary Key. Click on `Next`. Choose the file name and click on `Finish`.

10 Access creates a new table with the same name as the original text file, unless you choose to append data to an existing file. Choose `Close`.

Task 2: Importing delimited text files

Note: to complete this exercise you need access to a copy of an appropriate word processing package, such as Word for Windows.

Create a delimited text file into which you can enter data that matches the **Classes** table. If you are working with Word for Windows you may choose to do this by creating a table but you will need to convert the table to text before saving as a **.txt** file. Text delimited by commas or tabs may be saved directly as a **.txt** file. Save this file as ***Classes3***. As in FIGURE 36.2, enter the field names in the first row, and then enter some records for specific classes, one record per row, as required.

Class No	Class Day	Class Time	Class Tutor	Class Activity	Male/Female /Mixed
26	Tuesday	14.00	Miss Bates	Badminton	Female
27	Tuesday	15.00	Miss Bates	Badminton	Female
28	Wednesday	09.00	Mr Flowers	Multi-gym	Mixed
29	Thursday	21.00	Mr Tonks	Multi-gym	Male

1   Open Access and open the Database window.

2   Choose **File-Get External Data-Import**.

3   In the File of type list box in the **Import** dialog box choose the appropriate format for the data that you want to import (e.g. text files) and the drive and directory that contain the file to be imported.

4   Select the text file to be imported and then choose the **Import** button. The **Text Import Wizard** dialog box will be displayed.

5   Choose Delimited as the format. Click on **Next**.

6   Specify the Text Delimiter that has been used, e.g. Comma or Tab.

7   Tick the 'First row contains field names' check box. Click on Next.

8   Specify that you would like to store your data in a new table.

9   Accept the data types for the fields. Click on **Next**.

10 Set **Class No** as the primary key and name the new table *Classes3*. Click on **Finish**.

11 View this table in Datasheet view, and then in Design view. Change the data and data type of **Class Time** to a time format.

Notes

We have just explored a further way of creating text and entering it in a database. Normally it is more satisfactory to enter data directly into a database, but on occasions an existing word processed file, say, in this instance, of the classes on offer, or the names and addresses of some members, may usefully be incorporated into an Access database, either simply so that it is merged with other similar data, or because it is easier to sort, group and query the data in database format.

We do not describe importing fixed-width text fields here.

Exporting a table

What you will learn in this unit

Data can be exported from Access tables to text files, spreadsheets or to any of the database formats from which importing can be executed. Data can also be exported to a Word for Windows mail merge data file, which can then be used to create form letter, mailing labels and other merged documents. Data may be exported to other database applications so that it can be merged with other data in other files.

At the end of this unit you will be able to:

- export a table to a database
- export a table to a spreadsheet
- export a table to a word processor.

Understanding exporting

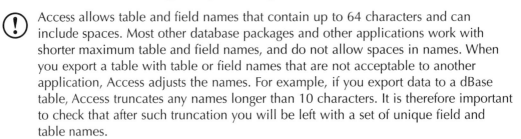

Access allows table and field names that contain up to 64 characters and can include spaces. Most other database packages and other applications work with shorter maximum table and field names, and do not allow spaces in names. When you export a table with table or field names that are not acceptable to another application, Access adjusts the names. For example, if you export data to a dBase table, Access truncates any names longer than 10 characters. It is therefore important to check that after such truncation you will be left with a set of unique field and table names.

To export data in a table to a file in a format that other applications can use:

1 Display the Database window.

2 Choose **File-Save As/Export.**

3 In the **Save As** dialog box choose 'To an external File or Database'. Click on **OK** .

4 Choose the drive and directory in which you wish to save the file.

5 Select the type of file to be created from the 'Save as type' list box and give this version of the table an appropriate filename (FIGURE 37.1). Click on **Export** .

FIGURE 37.1

Exporting to a database or spreadsheet file

To export data to a database or spreadsheet file:

1 Open the database containing the table that you wish to export and select the table.

2 Choose **File-Save As/Export**. In the **Save As** dialog box choose 'To an external File or Database'. Click on **OK**.

3 Choose the drive and directory in which you wish to save the file

4 Select the type of database file to be created from the 'Save as type' list box and give this version of the table an appropriate filename. Click on **Export**.

Task 1: Exporting a table to dBase or FoxPro

Note: To complete this task you require either dBase or FoxPro on your system. dBase field names are only 10 characters long so you may need to revise your Access field names.

 Export the table that was imported in Unit 35, **Classes**:

1 Switch to the database containing the table **Classes** and highlight it.

2 Choose **File-Save As/Export**. In the **Save As** dialog box choose 'To an external File or Database'. Click on **OK**.

3   Choose the drive and directory in which you wish to save the file

4   Select the type of dBase or FoxPro file to be created from the 'Save as type' list box and give this version of the table the name ***Classes4***. Click on **Export** .

Task 2: Exporting a table to a spreadsheet

Note: to complete this task you require a spreadsheet package such as Excel or Lotus 1-2-3.

1   Export the table that was imported earlier, **Classes**, following the same steps as in Task 1 but this time selecting, say, Excel as the file type.

2   Enter the name of the file to where you want the data exported as ***Classes5***.

Exporting a table to a text file

It may often be appropriate to select a set of records from a table and export them to a word processor for further formatting or for integration into a text-based document.

To export an Access table to a text file:

1 Open the database containing the table that you wish to export and select the table.

2 Choose **File-Save As/Export**. In the **Save As** dialog box choose 'To an external File or Database'. Click on **OK** .

3 Choose the drive and directory in which you wish to save the file

4 Select a text file type from the 'Save as type' list box and give this version of the table an appropriate filename. Click on **Export** .

Task 3: Exporting a table to a text file

Suppose we wish to create a brochure detailing the opportunities for ladies' leisure and recreational activities available at Chelmer Leisure and Recreation Centre. This leaflet will essentially be a word processed document containing text about the activities and the centre. However, embedded in the document will be a list of keep fit and multi-gym classes for ladies. In order to extract this information from our **Access Classes** table and insert the data into the leaflet we first need to select the appropriate records by the use of a query, then we need to convert the result of the query to a table, and then export the data in the table to a word processor file.

To execute the query:

1   Click on the Queries tab in the Database window and click on the **New** button to create a new query.

2   In the **Show Table** dialog box, choose **Classes**. Click on **Close** .

3   Add the appropriate fields to the query.

4   Use criteria to select the required records.

5   Display the dynaset.

6   Choose **Query-Make Table**. Key in a suitable name for the table. Click on **OK** .

7   Click on the **Run** button and a message box will display the number of records that are being added to the new table. Click on **Yes** to create the new table.

To export the data to a word processor file:

8   Click on the **Tables** tab and select the newly created table.

9   Choose **File-Save As/Export**. Access displays the **Save As** dialog box. In the **Save As** dialog box choose 'To an external File or Database'. Click on **OK** .

10 Choose the drive and directory in which you wish to save the file.

11 Select a text file type from the 'Save as type' list box and choose an appropriate filename. Click on **Export** .

Exporting Access data to another Access database

Exporting and importing are two sides of the same process. Data can be transferred between Access databases, either by importing or exporting. You import when the current database is the database where you need a copy of the table or other object, and you export when you are in the database that contains the object or data you want copied to another database.

To export a table or other database object, follow the steps for exporting a table but to select an object other than a table click on the appropriate tab in the Database window.

After exporting the object is in both databases and there is no link between the two copies of the object, so, for example, if the object is updated in one database it will not be updated in another.

Using the clipboard to transfer data

What you will learn in this unit

In addition to transferring data between Access and other applications by importing, attaching and exporting data, information can be transferred between applications using the clipboard. Transferring data using the clipboard is very straightforward, provided the data is in an acceptable format. It is especially easy if you are working with Excel and Word alongside Access. At the end of this unit you will be able to:

■ use the clipboard to transfer data.

Using the clipboard to transfer data

The clipboard is the temporary area where Windows can store information from any applications designed to use it. The basic procedure is to:

1 Select the data to be moved.

2 Select **Edit-Copy** or **Edit-Cut**, depending upon whether you also wish to retain the data in its original location or not.

3 Switch to the application into which you wish to import data.

4 Select **Edit-Paste**.

This procedure can be adopted, for example, for:

■ moving Access data into an Excel (or other) spreadsheet

■ moving Access data into a Word for Windows document in the form of a table

■ moving Access objects from one database to another.

Task 1: Using the clipboard to move Access data into a Word document

Chelmer Leisure and Recreation Centre may find it useful to have a list of those members who are children or, in other words, have a membership category of Junior or Junior Club. First we need to create a query to select appropriate records, and then we can select appropriate records on the screen and use **Edit-Copy** and **Edit-Paste** to insert those records into a word processed document.

To create a query:

1 Click on the Queries tab in the Database window and click on the New button to create a new query.

2 In the **Show Table** dialog box, choose **Membership**. Click on **Add** and then **Close** .

3 Add the following fields to the query: **Membership Category**, **Firstname**, **Lastname**, **Date of Birth**, **Date of Joining**, **Sporting Interests**, **Sex**.

4 Use a criterion in the **Membership Category** field to select categories 3 OR 4.

5 Display the dynaset. Select the dynaset.

6 Copy the selection to the clipboard, switch to the word processor and paste the table from the clipboard.

Another case where Chelmer Leisure and Recreation Centre would wish to move Access data into a document would be to create a list of classes intended for a publicity document such as a poster or leaflet.

To create a query:

1 Click on the **Queries** tab in the Database window and click on the **New** button to create a new query.

2 In the **Show Table** dialog box, choose **Classes**. Click on **Add** and then **Close** .

3 Add the following fields to the query: **Class Day**, **Class Time**, **Class Activity**, **Male/Female/Mixed**.

4 Display the dynaset. Select the dynaset.

5 Copy the selection to the clipboard, switch to the word processor and paste the table from the clipboard.

How could you amend the query to produce a leaflet targeted at male members?

Task 2: Using the clipboard to move Access data into an Excel spreadsheet

This task investigates how bookings table data can be pasted into an Excel spreadsheet to perform additional analysis.

1 Create a query based on the **Bookings** table.

2 Add the fields **Booking No** and **Date**.

3 Click on the **Totals** button to create totals.

4 Select Count for Booking No and Group by for Date.

5   Use **Edit-Select All Records** and **Edit-Copy**.

6   Switch to Excel

7   Use **Edit-Paste** and the data is pasted in Excel.

The average number of bookings per day can be found, which could have been done using Access. However, Excel could be used to calculate the median and mode of this data. Other more sophisticated statistical analysis could be used on Access data transferred to Excel, such as forecasting using a linear regression technique.

Creating and editing macros

What you will learn in this unit

This unit introduces macros. A macro is basically a list of instructions, rather like a short program. When using Access, there may be occasions when the same series of actions is performed again and again. To save time these actions may be recorded as a macro so that one command, to run the macro, can replace the need to issue a series of commands.

By performing a series of actions macros can automate your database application. Macros in Access are powerful and perform many tasks that in other database management systems could only be achieved by writing a program. Creating macros, however, does require a clear understanding of your database application so that you can plan exactly what you want each macro to do. In this and the following four units, you will be introduced to some macros, which, while not being comprehensive, should cover some of the basics. This unit shows you how to:

■ create simple macros.

The macro window

Macros are entered in macro windows, just as you enter a query using a query window or a form using a form window.

The macro window is usually shown with two columns, Action and Comment, as illustrated in FIGURE 39.1. In the Action column the action for the macro is selected, the action being selected from a drop-down list associated with that cell. In the Comments column you can add comments to act as a reminder of the function of the macro.

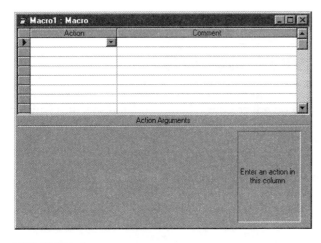

FIGURE 39.1

Task 1: A macro to open a form

This macro is easy to create and is one that is used frequently. This task considers construction of the macro stage by stage. At each stage relevant explanation is given.

1   Click on the **Macros** tab in the Database window and click on the **New** button to display the macro window.

The first action of this macro is OpenForm. There are many actions to choose from, as you will discover when you open the list box of the Action cell.

2   Open the **Action** cell list box. Scroll through the actions and select the OpenForm action.

When you do this you will see that an argument section appears in the lower left of the macro window. Whatever action is selected, there will nearly always be an argument section to complete. Some actions require more arguments than others. Refer to the section on 'Understanding actions and arguments'.

3   Open the **Form Name** list in the **Action Arguments** section and select **Membership**. Leave the action arguments as their default values.

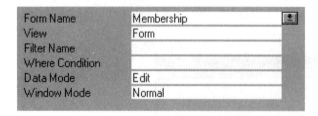

The View argument opens the form in form run mode. The Data Mode argument of Edit allows the form to be edited. The Where Condition specifies which record is displayed when the form opens. If this argument is left blank then the form is opened displaying the first record.

4   Key into the **Comment** column the description ***Open Membership form.***

5   Save the macro with the name ***Chelmer***.

Note: a macro must be saved before it can be run or executed. Choose **File-Save** or press *F12* to save the macro. In the **Save As** dialog box type a descriptive name for the macro. Click on **OK**.

6   The macro can be tested by running it. Click on the **Run** button on the toolbar. The **Membership** form should be displayed with the first record showing.

 Note: there are several different ways in which a macro can be run or executed. Refer to the section on *Executing macros* for details of the different methods.

7   Close the form and close the macro. The macro name should be displayed in the Database window.

Modifying a macro

A macro may need to be edited to change its actions or to correct an error. All or part of a macro may be copied from one macro window to another to save having to repeat work that has already been done. Macros may be copied from one database to another.

Normally a macro is edited to change its actions, usually to improve or refine them. Display the macro window that you wish to modify. Editing may be achieved using either the mouse or the keyboard.

Task 2: Editing a macro

In this task the macro created in Task 1 will be opened and edited so that when it opens the **Membership** form it displays the form ready to accept a new record. This is useful when a new member's details are to be entered.

1   Open the macro **Chelmer** in design mode.

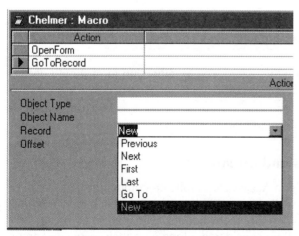

2   For the second action of the macro select the GoToRecord action.

3   To define which record to go to, the Record argument is used. Open the list box associated with this argument and select New.

4   Save the macro and run it. This time the **Membership** form should be displayed ready to accept a new record.

5   Close the form and the macro.

Task 3: Sizing and positioning the form

To add a further refinement to the macro to open the form, the size of the form can be set. If the size is not set then the form will be displayed at the last size used when the form was displayed in design mode. Sizing and positioning a form from a macro gives consistency to your database application.

1   Open the macro **Chelmer** in design mode.

2   Insert a row in the macro sheet below the OpenForm action. Highlight the second row and use **Insert-Row** to insert a blank row.

3   In the new row select the action **MoveSize**. Set the arguments as shown in the following table.

Right	The new horizontal position of the window's upper left corner, measured from the left edge of its containing window	4 cm
Down	The new vertical position of the window's upper left corner, measured from the top edge of its containing window	1 cm
Width	The window's new width	15 cm
Height	The window's new height	12 cm

4   Save the macro and run it.

5   You may need to adjust the sizes in the MoveSize arguments to suit your form. To do this close the **Membership** form, then edit and save the macro.

6   Save the changes and run the macro. The **Membership** form should display nicely and be ready to accept a new record.

7   Close the **Membership** form and the macro.

Understanding actions and arguments

The macro actions available in Access can duplicate commands that would be chosen from the menus as well as control many processes such as synchronising the records that forms display. There are many actions available, so by means of illustration a few actions will be considered, along with their associated arguments.

If the action duplicates a command that would generate a dialog box then the arguments are the selections that would be made in that dialog box. Three of the many actions are illustrated below:

Action	Argument	Function
FindRecord	Find What Match Match Case Search Search As Formatted Only Current Field Find First	Finds the next record after the current record meeting the specified criteria. Searches through a table, form or dynaset.
OpenForm	Form Name View Filter Name Where Condition Data Mode Window Mode	Opens or activates a form in one of its views.
OpenReport	Report Name View Filter Name Where Condition	Opens a report in the view specified and filters the records before printing.

By defining the arguments, for example, the name of a report in the Report Name argument, then the appropriate action is carried out.

Executing macros

You can run a macro in many ways. If you are creating quick macros for immediate use, you may want to run them by choosing them from the macro window or the database window. To create a system that is more automated or one that is easier to use, you can run a macro in a variety of ways, which are outlined briefly below and are discussed in more detail later.

Running from the macro window

A macro can be run from its macro window. This capability is useful for testing a macro. To run the macro, click on the **Run** button on the toolbar or choose **Run-Start**. If the active macro window contains a group of macros, only the first macro in the macro window runs. To run a specific macro in the group, see Unit 40.

From any window

Choose **Tools-Macro** and in the **Run Macro** dialog box select or key in the name of the macro. Click on **OK**.

From another macro

A macro can be run from another macro using the RunMacro action. The argument for this action is the name of the macro to be called. When the called macro has run Access returns control to the next action in the calling macro. The macro may run repeatedly if either the Repeat Count or Repeat Expression is set.

From an event

The running of a macro can be 'triggered' by an event. An event can be the opening or closing of a form or report or it can be the selecting of a control. For example, a macro which opens a form can run when a field is selected; a macro which validates an entry can run when a field is exited. These kind of macro events make your database application much more professional in operation.

From a button

This is another way to make your database application more professional. Command buttons are a very easy addition to a form. By clicking on the button the macro can be performed, such as opening another form.

From a shortcut key

It is a good idea to assign frequently used macros to a shortcut key, for example *Ctrl-p* could be assigned to a macro that performs printing. When you press the shortcut key combination the macro will run.

Creating macro groups

What you will learn in this unit

It is useful to keep related macros together, and Access offers the facility to group macros. Therefore, it is possible to have more than one macro in a macro window. This has the added advantage of reducing the number of macro windows. Many macros are small, only a few lines long, and if each required a separate macro window then it would be difficult to keep track of them all.

A macro can be assigned to a command button so that when the button is clicked the macro runs. Buttons may be added to existing forms based on tables or they can be added to blank forms. A blank form that does not have an associated table can be created. This type of form is known as an unbound from. By adding buttons to the form it can become a menu form.

By the end of this unit you will be able to:

- create a simple macro group

- add buttons to a form

- assign macros to the buttons.

Creating macro groups

To distinguish macros in one window, each has its own name. The macro name is entered in the Macro Name column of the window and this column is displayed by clicking on the **Macro Names** button in the toolbar or by choosing **View-Macro Names**. This column is displayed to the left of the Action column.

Each macro in the window begins with the action to the right of its name. The macro ends when it reaches the beginning of the next macro or runs out of actions. There is no need for a particular end action.

When a macro window contains several macros, then to refer to a specific macro within the group use the following syntax: ***macrowindowname.macroname***, where a full stop separates the macro window name from the macro name; for example, **Chelmer.NewBooking**. To run a particular macro in a group choose **Tools-Macro** and select the macro required from the drop-down list. Macro names are listed using the syntax described above. Note that if the macro name is omitted then the first macro in the group will run.

Task 1: Creating a macro group

In this task another macro will be added to the **Chelmer** macro. This will be another open form macro to open the booking form ready to take a new booking.

1   Display the **Chelmer** macro window.

2   Click on the **Macro Names** button on the toolbar.

3   Leave a couple of blank rows below the existing macro and in the Macro Name column put *NewBooking*.

4   On the next row select the action OpenForm. Set the Form Name argument to **Bookings**.

Macro Name	Action
	OpenForm
	GoToRecord
NewBooking	OpenForm
	GoToRecord

5   The second action is GoToRecord, with the argument of Record set to New.

6   Save the macro.

7   To run this part of the macro group select Tools-Macro.

8   In the Run Macro dialog box open the drop-down menu, select **Chelmer.NewBooking** and click on **OK** .

9   Close the form and close the macro.

Adding command buttons to a form

A macro can be made convenient to run by assigning it to a button on a form, either existing or blank. The button can then be clicked to run the macro.

1 Open the form in design view and display it by the side of the Database window.

2 Click the **Macros** tab in the Database window.

3 Drag the name of the macro onto the form where the button is to appear and release.

4 The button will have the name of the macro. If you wish, you can change this by editing the text on the button.

5 Save the form with the button.

6 Display the form in Run mode and click on the button to run the macro.

Task 2: Creating a blank form and adding buttons to it

In this task an unbound blank form will be created which will only contain two command buttons. The first command button to be added will be one which, when clicked, will open the **Membership** form ready to accept a new member's details. The second button will open the **Bookings** form ready to accept a new booking. To create a blank unbound form:

1   From the Database window click on the ▨ Forms ▨ tab and click on ▨ New ▨. Leave the 'Choose the table or query...' box empty as this form is not bound to a table or query. Choose Design View.

2   To add a command button, display the new blank form and the Database window side by side.

3   Click on the Macro tab of the Database window and select **Chelmer**.

4   Drag the macro onto the form.
    A button appears with the name Chelmer on it.

5   The name on the button can be changed by editing the Caption property. Edit the name of the button to read *New Member*.
    You should find that the On Click property is set to Chelmer, i.e. the first macro in the macrogroup Chelmer will run when the button is clicked.

6   Set the properties of the form as follows (if the form is not selected use **Edit-Select Form** to select it):

Property	Setting
Caption	Form Menu (the name that will appear in the title bar of the form)
DefaultView	Single Form
ScrollBars	Neither
Record Selectors	No
Navigation buttons	No

7   Save the form as *Form Menu*. Run the form and click on the New Member button you have just created. Close the **Membership** form.

8   Return to Design view of the Form Menu form.

9   Drag the macro onto the form.
    A button appears with the name Chelmer on it.

10 The name on the button can be changed by editing the Caption property. Edit the name of the button to read *Make Booking.*

11 You should also edit the On Click property, which is set to **Chelmer**, to **Chelmer.NewBooking** so that the macro **Chelmer.NewBooking** will run when the button is clicked.

12 You may add a title and adjust fonts as illustrated below.

13 Save the form and try the new button.

Task 3: Adding a button to a form

This will be a very simple macro to close the open object, which might be a form or report. In the preceding task to close after adding a new member or taking a new booking would be simple if a button labelled Close were added to both the **Membership** and **Bookings** forms.

The macro to close an object is simple and it can be added to the **Chelmer** macro group. To add this macro:

1 Display the **Membership** form in design view.

Check that the **Control Wizard** button in the Toolbox is depressed.

2 Select the Command Button tool from the Toolbox and click at the bottom of the form.

The Command Button Wizard starts.

3 Select Form Operations from the Categories list and Close Form from the Actions list. Click on **Next>** .

4 Choose a picture or text for the button. Give the button the name **Close Membership Form** and click on **Finish** .

5 Save the form.

6 Try out the macro. Clicking on the **Close** button should close the form.

7 Add a **Close** button to both the **Bookings** form and the **Form Menu** form.

Notice that the button's On Click property is set to Event Procedure.

8 Save the forms and test your macros.

Assigning macros to keys

What you will learn in this unit

It is useful to be able to assign a frequently used macro to a keystroke because this gives the operator more choice when using the database. The example we shall consider is that of _Ctrl-n_ to display the Membership form ready to accept a new members record and _Ctrl-b_ to display the Booking form. Examples of other shortcut keys that could be used are _Crtl-x_ to close or _Crtl-p_ to print.

At the end of this unit you will be able to:

■ Assign macros to keys.

Assigning a macro to a key

A separate macro needs to be created in which the key assignments are set. All key assignments are kept in this macro as a group. So that Access knows that this is a key assignment macro, it is saved with the name **AutoKeys**. In the AutoKeys macro each key combination has a name, and this name must follow the naming convention shown in the table below:

Key combination	Macro name
Ctrl-letter	^_letter_
Ctrl-number	^_number_
Function key	{F1} and so on
Ctrl-Function key	^{F1} and so on
Shift-Function key	+{F1} and so on
Insert	{Insert}
Ctrl-Insert	^{Insert}
Shift-Insert	+{Insert}
Delete	{Delete} or {Del}
Ctrl-Delete	^{Delete} or ^{Del}
Shift-Delete	+{Delete} or +{Del}

To assign a macro to a shortcut key:

1 Create and save the macros and/or macro groups to which you wish to assign shortcut keys.

2 Open a new macro window and display the Macro Name column. This macro will become a macro group in which all shortcut keys are defined.

3 In the macro name column put the macro name, for example, **^p**.

4 The action for this macro will be a RunMacro action, which will refer to one of the macros you have already created. See the following section for more detail on the RunMacro action.

5 State the macro name that you are calling in the Macro Name argument. Use the correct syntax, i.e. if the macro is in a group then use **macrogroupname.macroname**.

6 Use the Comment column to note which macro is being called.

7 Save the shortcut key macro as AutoKeys.

8 Any shortcut keys you wish to set up later must be added to this macro.

The RunMacro action

A macro can be run from within another macro by using the RunMacro action. The arguments for the RunMacro action are the name of the macro to be run and the number of times the macro is to repeat. The macro may be set to repeat a set number of times or an expression can be used to test whether the macro has been performed the required number of times.

When the main (or calling) macro is run it performs its list of actions. When the RunMacro action is encountered the specified macro runs the required number of times. When that has finished Access returns control to the next action in the calling macro.

Task 1: Assigning shortcut keys

In this task the shortcut key *Ctrl-m* (^m) is to be assigned to the macro that opens the **Membership** form ready to accept a new member's record and *Ctrl-b* (^b) to opening the **Bookings** form. To create an **AutoKeys** macro:

1 Open a new macro sheet. Display the Macro Name column.

2 Put **^m** in the Macro Name column.

3 In the **Action** column select the RunMacro action and set the Macro Name argument to **Chelmer** (this is the first macro of the Chelmer group of macros).

4 In the Comments column put *Opens Membership form for new record*.

5 In the next row of the Macro Name column put **^b**.

6   In the Action column select the RunMacro action and set the Macro Name argument to **Chelmer.NewBooking** (this is the **NewBooking** macro of the **Chelmer** group of macros).

7   In the Comments column put ***Opens Bookings form for new record***.

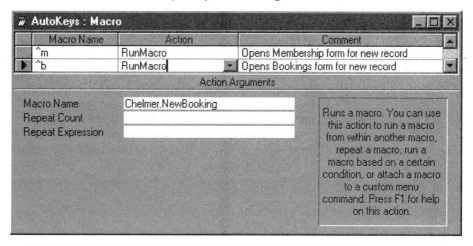

8   Save the macro as ***AutoKeys***.

9   Open the Form menu and try using the shortcut key.

You may have noticed that in many Windows applications the shortcut letter in a menu or on a button is underlined. It is possible to do this by displaying the form or report containing the button in design mode and editing the caption so that an '&' precedes the letter to be underlined. For example, Make Booking would be typed as ***Make &Booking*** so that it appeared as Make Booking on the button.

Assigning macros to events

What you will learn in this unit

Specific events in forms and reports can be used to 'trigger' the running of a macro. Examples of events are the opening of a form, the user selecting or exiting from a field control or the user double-clicking on a field.

By assigning macros to events, you can make your database system more professional as set procedures within the system become automated. Event-driven macros can be used to open multiple forms together, to print reports using specific queries, or to create error checks that are more extensive than those available through control properties. There are more form events than report events.

At the end of this unit, you will be able to:

■ assign a macro to an event

■ use conditions to determine how a macro will run

■ use control reference syntax correctly

■ appreciate that more complex procedures can be achieved using small program modules.

The events for a form or report can be found in the table of properties. Forms, controls and reports have different events associated with them. The following tables illustrate some of the events to which macros can be assigned.

Events in a form or record:

Form property	Event	Example of use
On Open	Runs the macro when the form opens but before displaying a record	The macro may open or close other forms when the form opens
Before Insert	Runs the macro when the user begins to enter data into a new record	The macro can display extra information or a warning message
Before Update	Runs the macro after the user has finished changing or entering the record but before the record is updated in the database	The macro can display a dialog box asking the user to confirm that the record be updated
After Update	Runs the macro after the user has finished changing or entering the record but after the record has been updated in the database	The macro can update other forms using the data in the new record

Form property	*Event*	*Example of use*
On Delete	Runs the macro when the user deletes a record but before the record is actually deleted	The macro may ask for confirmation as to whether the record should be deleted
On Close	Runs the macro as the form is about to close but has not disappeared from the screen	The macro may ask whether data may be transferred when the form is closed

Events in a form control:

Form control property	*Event description*	*Example of use*
On Enter	Runs the macro when a control is clicked, i.e. just as it receives the focus	The macro may ask for a password before allowing data entry
On Click	Runs the macro when a command button is clicked	The caption on the button usually indicates the function of the macro, for example Print
Before Update	Runs the macro after the user leaves a control but before the control is changed	The macro can validate the data that has been entered and ask for it to be corrected
On Dbl Click	Runs the macro when the user double-clicks on a control or its label	Can display a form with information regarding data entry
On Exit	Runs the macro when the user attempts to move to another control but before the focus moves away	Can define the next control using the GoToControl action.

Events in a report:

Report event	*Event description*	*Example of use*
On Open	Runs the macro when the report opens but before printing	Displays a form in which to enter criteria

To assign a macro to an event, first create and save the macro. To assign it to the required form, report or control:

1 Open the required form or report in design view.

2 Select the form, report or control to which the macro is to be assigned.

241

To...	Do this
Select a form or report	Click on the background in a form. Click outside a report section. Choose either **Edit-Select Form** or **Edit-Select Report**
Select a report section	Click on the section header
Select a control	Click on the control

3 Display the properties window by clicking on the Properties button in the toolbar.

4 Select the required event in the properties table.

5 Open the combo box and select the macro name to be assigned to this event. If the macro is part of a group, select the group's name and edit it to add a dot and the name of the macro.

6 Save the changes made and test the macro.

Using conditions

Your macros can have the capability to make decisions about how they operate. Macros can test whether a condition is true, and when that condition is true they can run actions you specify.

By adding the condition column to the macro window, expressions can be added. In this column, you enter expressions that can be evaluated as true or false. If the expression is true the macro action on its right runs; if false the macro action does not run.

Expressions test the values of control names, for example:

■ [Surname]="Smith": True when Surname control contains the text **Smith**.

■ [Membership Fee]<20: True when the control **Membership Fee** is less than 20.

Task 1: Using conditions to control the focus in a form

In this task a macro will be assigned to the **Member/Class** control in the **Bookings** form which will control whether the focus moves to the **Membership No** control or to the **Class No** control.

1   Create the macro group **Booking** as illustrated. There are two macros in the group and they are named after the controls to which they will be assigned.

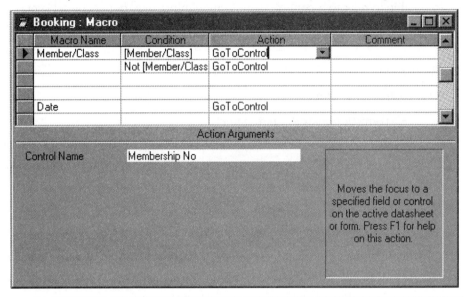

2   The **Member/Class** macro has two conditions, one if the **Member/Class** control is true and the other if the **Member/Class** control is false. If the **Member/Class** control is true then the GoToControl action specifies **Membership No** (as illustrated). If the **Member/Class** control is false then the GoToControl action specifies **Class No**.

3   To move the focus to Date after either a Membership or Class number has been entered, the macro Date is used. This macro uses a GoToControl action with the Control Name argument **Date**.

4   Save the macro group as **Booking**.

5   Display the **Bookings** form in design mode.

6   Click on the **Member/Class** control and set the On Exit property to **Booking**. This means that the first macro in the macro group **Bookings** will run when this control is exited.

7   Set the On Exit control of **Membership No** to **Booking.Date**. Repeat for the **Class No** control.

8   Save the form and test the macro group by entering some data.

Control reference syntax

To be able to refer to a control name from within a macro, the correct syntax must be used. If the way in which the control is referred does not follow the rules of syntax then the macro will not work.

The syntax for referring to controls is as follows:

For a control on a form:

> Forms!*formname*!*controlname*

For a control on a report:

> Reports!*reportname*!*controlname*

For a control on a subform:

> Forms!*mainformname*!*subformname.Form*!*controlname*

If the name of the form, report or control contains spaces then it must be enclosed in square brackets; for example:

> Forms![Membership Category]![Membership Fee]

If the macro is run from the form or report containing the control then the control can be referred to by the controlname alone. This is known as the short syntax, for example:

> [Membership Fee]

If you are in doubt always use the full syntax. If the short syntax is used in an inappropriate situation then the macro will not run.

Task 2: Using a form to enter report criteria

If a report is created that is based on a query then it is useful to be able to enter criteria for the report. The report that is to be used is the one based on the **When joined** query, which listed members who had joined the centre during a defined time period. This query was created in Unit 12. Use Report Wizards to create a single-column report from this query. Save the report with the name **When joined**.

A form will be created that will allow the start and end dates of the time period to be entered before the report is previewed.

The task involves creating an unbound form, a macro group, a module and the underlying query, and the report will be edited. This is therefore a long task, so follow the steps carefully.

Step 1 is to create an unbound form:

1   From the Database window click on the **Forms** tab and click on **New**. Leave the 'Choose the table or query...' box empty as this form is not bound to a table or query.

2   Select **Design View** and click on `OK` .

3   In **Design View** set the properties for the form:

Property	Setting
Caption	Period under investigation (the name that will appear in the title bar of the form)
Default View	Single Form
Scroll Bars	Neither
Views Allowed	Form
Record Selectors	No
Navigation Buttons	No
Dividing Lines	No

4   Add an unbound text box for each criterion you want to enter. There are two criteria to be entered so add two text boxes.

Use the completed form illustrated below as a guide.

5   Set the properties for the text boxes as follows.

Property	Setting
Control Source	Start Date (first text box)
	End Date (second text box)
	Use a ControlName that describes the type of criterion.
Format	Short Date (both text boxes)
	Use a Format that reflects the data type of the criterion.

6   Edit the label of the first text box to read ***Period beginning*** and the second text box to read ***Period ending***, as illustrated below.

7   Add text to indicate the purpose of the form.

8   Save the form, and give it the name ***WHEN JOINED***.

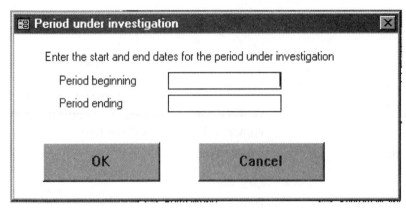

Your form will not look like this yet as you have only used design mode. The
OK and **Cancel** command buttons will be added to the form after you create
macros for them.

Step 2 is to create a module that is used by one of the macros.

Modules have not been introduced as they involve programming and it is not the
intention of this book to discuss programming Access other than superficially, as in
this example. The module being created is a function which will return either 'true'
or 'false' depending on whether a specified form is loaded. Access modules may be
standard, i.e. they are available globally, or they may be attached to a form or
report. In this case the function will be attached to the **When joined** report.

9 From the database window open the report **When joined** in design view. Click on
   the **Code** button on the toolbar to display a module window. Type the line:
   Function IsLoaded(MyFormName) and press *Enter*.

10 Key in the rest of the module exactly as illustrated below. The line End Function is
   preset and you add the lines in between. If you are familiar with Basic you will
   notice that a For... Next loop and an If statement are used to test the names of open
   forms against the name specified and to set the function to true if a match is found.

```
Report_When joined : Module                            _ □ ×
Object: (General)              ▼    Proc: IsLoaded                ▼
Function IsLoaded(MyFormName)
'Accepts: a form name
'Purpose: determines if the specified form has been loaded
'Returns: True if form is loaded, False if not
Dim i As Integer
    IsLoaded = False
    For i = 0 To Forms.Count - 1
        If Forms(i).Name = MyFormName Then
            IsLoaded = True
            Exit Function    'Quit function once form has been found
        End If
    Next
End Function
```

11 Close the window.

The function will be saved automatically as part of the report when the report design is saved.

Step 3 is to create the macros for the form.

The four macros used by the form will be kept in one macro group, as illustrated at the end of this step.

12 In the Database window, click the **Macros** tab, and then choose the **New** button.

13 Create a macro that opens the unbound **When joined** form. Display the Macro Names column. Give the macro the name *Open Dialog*, and select the OpenForm action.

14 Set the action arguments for OpenForm as follows:

Argument	Setting
Form Name	When joined
View	Form
Data Mode	Edit
Window Mode	Dialog

15 Add a second action that cancels previewing or printing the report.

16 Add a macro to the group that closes the form. Give the macro a name such as *Close Dialog*. Select the Close action. Set the action arguments as follows:

Argument	Setting
Object Type	Form
Object Name	When joined

17 Create a macro for the **OK** button. This macro hides the form. Give the macro a name, such as *OK*, and select the SetValue action. Then set its action arguments as follows:

Argument	Setting
Item	Visible
Expression	No

18 Create a macro for the **Cancel** button. This macro closes the form. Give the macro a name, such as *Cancel*, and select the Close action. Then set its action arguments as follows:

Argument	Setting
Object Type	Form
Object Name	When joined

19 Save and close the macro group. Give the macro group a name that reflects the general purpose of the group, in this case **When joined**.

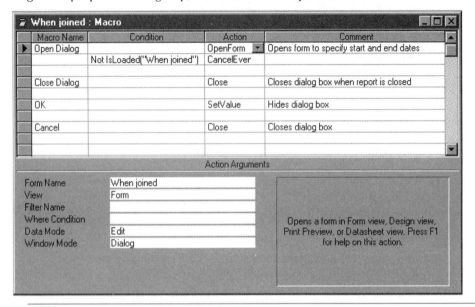

Step 4 is to add **OK** and **Cancel** command buttons to the form:

20 Re-open the unbound form **When joined** in Design View.

21 Using the toolbox, add a command button 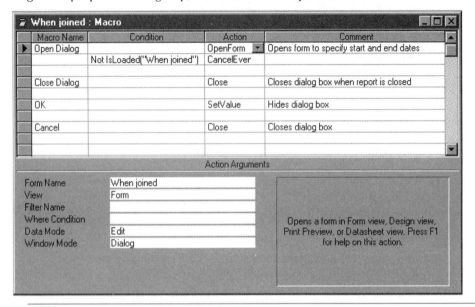 for **OK**, and set its properties as follows:

Property	Setting
Caption	OK
On Click	When joined.OK (macrogroup.macroname)

22 Add a command button for Cancel, and set its properties as follows:

Property	Setting
Caption	Cancel
On Click	When joined.Cancel

23 Save and close the form.

Step 5 is to edit the criteria in the underlying query **When joined**:

23 Open the **When joined** query in Design View.

24 Replace the criteria for the **Date of Joining** field. In the new criteria expression, the controls in the **When joined** form are used. Enter the following replacement expression to refer to controls named Start Date and End Date:

Between [Forms]![When joined]![Start Date] And [Forms]![When joined]![End Date]

25 Save the changes and close the query.

Step 6 is to attach the macros to the **When joined** report:

26 In Design View of the main report, set the following properties:

Property	Setting
On Open	When joined.Open Dialog
	(Name of the macro that opens the unbound When joined form)
On Close	When joined.Close Dialog
	(Name of the macro that closes the unbound When joined form)

27 Try putting two unbound controls into the header so that the title reads **List of members who joined between Start date and End date**.

Macros for data validation

What you will learn in this unit

When a table is defined it is possible to set Validation Rules to validate data being entered. One rule used in a previous unit prevented a Category No greater than six being entered, as there are only six categories of membership. Validation rules are limited in the validation that they can perform and macros can take validation one stage further. This unit demonstrates the use of macros for data validation. At the end of this unit, you will be able to:

- use macros for data validation

- run a start-up macro

- use macros to amend records.

Using macros for data validation

The kind of validation that a macro can perform is to check whether a member signing for a class is the right gender for that class. This will be considered in the following task. Another validation that could be performed is checking that a room is available at a certain day and time before a booking is accepted.

Task 1: Validating bookings for classes

This task uses a macro that will check whether a person booking a class is of the right gender. It will prevent a female member booking into a male class and vice versa. When a booking is made the **Class Lists** main/subform is used. The membership number is entered into the subform (**Class Member List**). To check whether the member is male or female, the membership data needs to be accessed. This can be done by opening the **Membership** form at the record of the membership number just entered.

To prevent the **Membership** form from displaying on the screen it can be opened as hidden by a validation macro that is assigned to the Before Update property of the **Class Member List Form**. To create this validation macro:

1   In the Database window, click the **Macros** tab, and then choose the **New** button.

2 Select the **OpenForm** action, then set the action arguments for **OpenForm** as follows:

Argument	Setting
Form Name	Membership
View	Form
Where Condition	[Membership No]=Forms![Class Lists]![Class Member List].Form![Membership No]
Data Mode	Read Only
Window Mode	Hidden

3 Add a second action that displays a message box. This action will only take place if the member is male and the class is female only. Click the `Conditions` button, and type the following expression (in one line) in the **Condition** column:

Forms![Membership]![Sex] And
Forms![Class Lists]![Male/Female/Mixed]="Female"

4 Select **MsgBox** as the action for this condition being true. Set the properties for the message box as follows:

Argument	Setting
Message	This is a female-only class
Beep	Yes
Type	None
Title	Classes Validation

5 Add a third action that cancels the event. This action is also dependent upon the condition in the row above, and to indicate this an ellipsis (...) is put in the condition column. Select the **CancelEvent** action.

6 The fourth action undoes the current record; select **DoMenuItem** as the action and set its properties:

Argument	Setting
Menu Bar	Form
Menu Name	Edit
Command	Undo

7   Add a fifth action that displays a message box. This action will only take place if the member is female and the class is male only. Click the **Conditions** button, and type the following expression in the **Condition** column:
    Not Forms![Membership]![Sex] And
    Forms![Class Lists]![Male/Female/Mixed]="Male"

8   Select **MsgBox** as the action for this condition being true. Set the properties for the message box as follows:

Argument	Setting
Message	This is a male-only class
Beep	Yes
Type	None
Title	Classes Validation

9   Add a sixth action that cancels the event. This action is also dependent upon the condition in the row above, and to indicate this an ellipsis (...) is put in the condition column. Select the CancelEvent action.

10 Add a seventh action that undoes the current record (as fourth action).

11 The final action is Close. Set its arguments as follows:

Argument	Setting
Object Type	Form
Object Name	Membership form

12 Save the macro using the name ***Male Female Validation***.

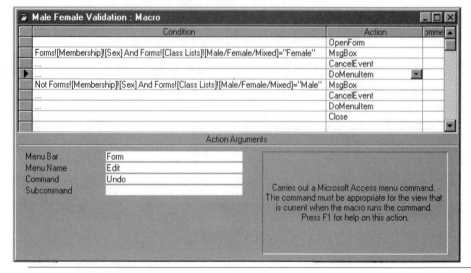

13 Open the **Class Member List** form in Design View. Display the form property sheet, open the Before Update property of the form (under the Event tab) and select Male Female Validation. Save and close the form.

14 Select the **Class Lists** main/subform and open it. Try entering a female member into a male class and vice versa to test your macro.

If it doesn't work it is likely that a name has been mistyped. Open the macro in design view and check it carefully.

Running a macro at start-up time

To give a database application a professional look a macro can be written that will run when the database is opened. This macro can open required forms and set any defaults. Typically a start-up macro would open a form displaying a main menu for the database. This might have various buttons that the user can click depending upon the action required.

The macro to perform the start-up tasks is written as usual, but to tell Access that it is the start-up macro it is saved with the name **Autoexec**. When the database is opened if there is a macro called **Autoexec** then it will be run.

It is possible to stop the macro **Autoexec** running if you wish to do some development work on the database, by holding down the *Shift* key when the OK button is clicked or *Enter* is pressed to open the database.

Using macros to create a record amendment form

Once a table has been created, such as the **Membership** table, it will need to be maintained. In this activity we consider the amendment of records. Members may, for example, change their address or category of membership or supply information not previously given. Records can be edited simply, when viewing the table, by using the Find facility to find the right record and then making changes to the field or fields in that record. However, this is not a particularly friendly interface, and a more sophisticated method is to create a form through which records can be located and amended. Such a form uses a list box displaying Membership numbers, through which the desired record may be selected. The following task will create an amendment form for the **Membership** table, as illustrated in FIGURE 43.1.

FIGURE 43.1

Task 2: Membership record amendment form

In this task a form and several small macros will be created.

1   Using AutoForm: Columnar, create a single-column form based on the **Membership** table. Give the form the title *Amend Membership Details Form*. Display the form in Design view and adjust the positions of the controls to allow room for the addition of the list box.

2   With the **Control Wizard** button in the toolbox depressed, click on the list box button and click on the form at the place where the list box is to go. In the **List Box Wizard** dialog box select the 'I want the list box to look up the values in a table or query' option. Click on **Next**.

3   Select the **Membership** table. Click on **Next**. Select **Membership No** by clicking on **>** and **Lastname** as columns in the list box. Click on **Next**. Remove the tick from the Hide key column check box as we are using the key to search for members. Now you may adjust the widths of the columns in the list box. Click on **Next** again and once more to accept that **Membership No** is the field to be used by the form. Edit the label of the list box to read *Select Membership No:* and click on **Finish**.

4 Display the property sheet for the list box control and give it the name **Select Membership No**.

5 You may wish to make further adjustments to the positions of the controls on the form. When finished, save the form as **Amend Membership Details**. Close the form.

6 Open the macro **Chelmer** in design view. Scroll down to the end of the existing macros and add a new one with the name **Find Record**. This macro has the following actions.

Action	Argument
GoToControl	Membership No
FindRecord	= [Select Membership No]
GoToControl	Select Membership No

7 Save the macro. Open the form **Amend Membership Details** in design view. Click on the list box, display its property sheet and assign the macro, **Chelmer.FindRecord** to the list box's After Update property. Save and close the form.

8 Add another macro, **Amend Member Load**, to the **Chelmer** macro group. This macro has just one action:

Action	Argument
GoToControl	Select Membership No

9 Close and save the macro group. Open the **Amend Membership Details** form again, in design view. Use **Edit-Select Form** and display the form's property sheet. Assign the macro **Chelmer.AmendMemberLoad** to the On Load property of the form.

10 Click on the **Membership No** control and set its Tab Stop property to No. Also set its Locked property to Yes.

11 Save the form. Try it out to search for member's records and make some changes. As a finishing touch you could add a **Close** button to this form.

You should find this form useful to search for records providing you know the member's membership number. If you only have a name then you will need to display the table and use the Find facility.

Integrative tasks

The following tasks draw on this and the previous four units concerning the use of macros.

Task 3: A report menu

This task creates a form containing several buttons which when clicked will preview a certain report. The underlying macro for each button opens a report, an action similar to that for opening a form.

1 Display the **Chelmer** macro window.

2 In the next convenient row put **Membership Report** as the name of this macro.

3 Open the Action cell list box. Scroll through the actions and select the **OpenReport** action. Set the arguments for this action as follows:

Argument	Setting
Report Name	Members2
View	Print Preview

4 Key into the Comment column the description **Preview Membership Report**.

5 Save the macro group.

6 In a similar fashion create macros to open the **Mailing**, **Classes4** and **Bookings** reports.

7 Create a blank unbound form. Add to it a title, e.g. **Reports Menu**, and add four buttons, one for each macro just created.

8 Label each button and assign the appropriate macro to it. Remember to use the right syntax, e.g. **Chelmer.Mailing** for the On Click property. Save the form as **Reports Menu** and run it.

Task 4: A query menu

This task creates a form containing several buttons which when clicked will run a certain query. The underlying macro for each button opens a report, an action similar to that for opening a form.

1 Display the **Chelmer** macro window.

2 In the next convenient row put **Sporting Interests** as the name of this macro.

3   Open the Action cell list box. Scroll through the actions and select the
    OpenQuery action. Set the argument for this action as follows (leave the others at
    their default settings):

Argument	*Setting*
Query Name	Members sporting interests

4   Key into the **Comment** column the description ***Sporting Interests Query***.

5   Save the macro group.

6   In a similar fashion, create macros to open the **Member Ages**, **Fitness Suite
    Bookings** and **When joined** queries.

7   Create a blank unbound form. Add to it a title, e.g. ***Queries Menu***, and add four
    buttons, one for each macro just created.

8   Label each button and assign the appropriate macro to it. Remember to use the
    right syntax, e.g. **Chelmer.Sporting Interests** for the On Click property. Save the
    form as ***Query Menu*** and run it.

A database application

What you will learn in this unit

In the earlier units we explored the creation and use of tables, queries, reports, forms and macros. In order to create a fully operational database system, known as an application, it is necessary to link all of these components together. In this unit we explore some of the issues associated with the creation of a working application. At the end of this unit you should:

■ understand the issues and stages in the design of an application

■ be able to use forms and macros to create a series of linked menus

■ be able to create a simple application for the use and maintenance of one table

■ appreciate the complexity of relational database design.

A major underlying objective of this unit is to attempt to begin to draw the various components of the Chelmer database that you have created in this book into a partial application. In order to retain this integrative focus, this unit, unlike most others in this book, will not seek to explore the wide range of features that can be used in the design of applications, such as drop-down menus, menu bars and pop-up forms, but will instead use some of the basic features and focus on the integration of the database components into a basic application, which the reader is welcome to refine later.

Understanding applications

Why do we need applications? Earlier units have introduced you to the creation of the component parts of applications: tables, forms, reports, queries and macros. (Modules might also be included in an application but we have not attempted these in this material.) You may think that you have already created an application! Indeed, through the Database window you are able to select tables, call up a form, edit data in tables, perform queries on tables and produce reports. This might be adequate for a relatively small personal or in-house database, but real applications are tailored for specific environments. A leisure management system would not access the database components through the Database window. Users expect to start the system up, and view a main menu which offers them one or a series of options, such as adding a new member or making a booking. The user does not want to have to remember the name of the table that needs to be accessed in order to perform these actions. The user expects to be able to click on a button or choose a menu option and move straight into the form that allows the appropriate data entry. So, for example, an opening or main menu screen might appear as in FIGURE 44.1.

FIGURE 44.1

When the user clicks on the first option a form, such as **Bookings** would be displayed. Clicking on System Maintenance would display an additional menu, which would offer further options, perhaps as displayed in FIGURE 44.2.

FIGURE 44.2

259

Clicking on one of these buttons would, for instance, lead to a further menu for the actions that can be performed on the **Membership** table, as, for example, in FIGURE 44.3.

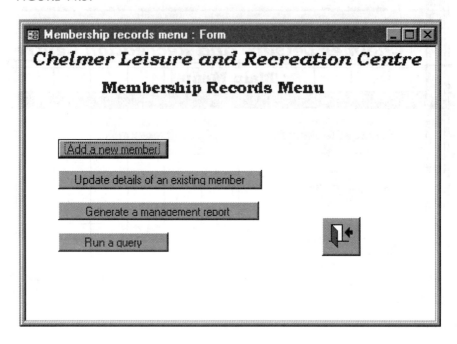

FIGURE 44.3

What, then, is a database application? The Access *User's Guide* offers a succinct definition:

> A Database Application is a set of related Microsoft Access database objects that you can use to accomplish a particular database task. For example, if you use a certain set of forms and reports frequently, you can create an application that gives you easy access to these forms and reports and displays them conveniently in the Microsoft Access window.

In Units 39 to 43 you developed some simple macros that could be used with forms and reports. You can use macros to create an application, or custom workspace, and to add features to your application. For example, you can create custom menu bars for forms, assign common actions to menu commands or key combinations, and automate various tasks such as printing daily reports or backing up your database.

Note: we have created the database components first and are now proceeding to integrate them into one application. This is not the way these things should be done! However, it is easier for the beginner to start to understand some of the components before attempting to integrate those components. If we were designing a database application for real, the same data analysis that led to the table design as shown in FIGURE 8.1 should consider the way in which that data is to be used. This would determine which forms, reports, queries, macros and modules were necessary and the function of each of these.

Task 1: Understanding applications

FIGURE 44.3 shows a menu for adding records to the **Membership** table. Draw on paper a similar menu for adding data to the **Classes** table. Indicate which of the forms and reports that you have already created might be accessed via this menu.

Creating a simple application

The sample application illustrated in the figures in this unit is extremely simplistic. For example, only forms are used for the display of menus, and windows, pull-down menus, menu bars and pop-up forms are not used. Yet even these simple menus start to illustrate some important features of good application design.

Screen design in an application is a type of form design, and all of the same design considerations must be taken into account. For example, it is important to choose easily legible fonts and font sizes, and to create an uncluttered screen.

Design must depend upon the application. In particular, the sequencing of the screen should make it easy to run through a normal task sequence, and it should be easy to move between related but distinct tasks.

Most systems have three types of users: systems managers (who have responsibility for maintaining the system, managers (seeking management reports and summary data) and operators (who, for example, are on the desk taking bookings, meeting members and answering members' enquiries). These users seek to perform different operations using the system. Menus and menu options must be grouped in such a way that different users find their applications easily accessible. Hence, for example, in FIGURE 44.1, the Main Menu for the Chelmer database, it is easy to go straight into desk functions such as making a booking, but other functions that might be more useful to managers are 'hidden' under System Maintenance. An additional refinement would be that workstations on the bookings desk did not display the System Maintenance options at all. This would lend greater security on workstations that were in a public access area.

A real system based on multiple tables is very complex to create and would involve much more input than you would probably wish to pursue. Instead, in Task 2 we create a small application based solely on the **Membership** table, and using some of the forms and reports that we have already created, as well as some special forms that will display the menus.

Task 2: Creating the main or opening menu for the membership table

We wish to create the Main Menu for the Chelmer Leisure and Recreation Centre as in FIGURE 44.1. The process has two stages: the creation of the form, and the creation of and linking of macros to the form. Where possible we use macros that were created in Units 39 to 43.

First to create a form:

1 Open a new form and stretch it.

2 Add a form header and footer.

3   Open the form header and insert the title text shown in FIGURE 44.1

4   Open the Detail band and insert the buttons as in FIGURE 44.1

5   Save the form as **Main Menu**.

6   Next, review and create appropriate macros. Macros similar to those required have already been created in Units 39–43. We need:

Button	Macro
Make a Booking	Opens a booking form (e.g. **Booking**), such as **NewBooking**
Check a Booking	Opens a booking form at the first record, ready for the user to search using **Edit-Find**
Add a New Member	Opens a form, such as **Membership**
System Maintenance	Opens a form, e.g. **System Maintenance Menu**
Close	Closes the active window

7   When you have checked that you have all of the above macros, open the form again in Design View.

8   Add the macros to the buttons in turn, by clicking on the button and inserting the macro name as the On Click property on the properties sheet.

Task 3: Creating the system maintenance menu

Using a similar approach to that used in Task 2, create the System Maintenance Menu shown in FIGURE 44.2.

Task 4: Creating the management reports menu

The Report Menu can be created using similar principles to those outlined in Task 2 in Unit 43. Try modifying the menu that you created in that task to look like this:

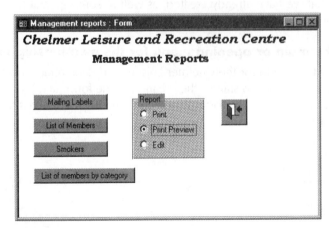

Integrative tasks

The following tasks call upon application design skills introduced in this unit.

Task 5: Creating the queries menu

Design a Membership Queries Menu which is consistent with the other menus that you have designed and which displays the following data:

Chelmer Leisure and Recreation Centre
Membership Queries Menu
New Query
Existing Query

Task 6: Designing a Bookings table main menu

1   Design a Bookings Main Menu for the **Bookings** table which is similar to that for the **Membership** table.

2   What is wrong with this menu for the person on the bookings desk?

   Think about the functions that this person would need to perform. Think about the questions that customers might ask, for which they would need to provide an answer.

3   Which, if any, of these functions might require the user to have access to data in other tables in the database?

4   Could customers make their own bookings through a system with the main menu in FIGURE 44.1? What additional security might be advisable?

Basic Windows operations

You may not be familiar with Windows, and Access may well be one of the first Windows products encountered by you. If you have not previously used Windows you are strongly recommended to run through the Windows tutorial, which introduces users to mouse techniques and the basic operation of Windows. This tutorial can be found by clicking on Start, selecting **Help**, clicking on the **Contents** tab, and selecting Tour: Ten minutes to using Windows. This appendix briefly summarises some of the key operations and should act as a ready reference to some of the terminology that is used elsewhere in the book.

Mouse techniques

The basic mouse techniques are listed in the table below, with a simple description of each technique:

To...	Do this
Point	Position the mouse pointer on or next to something.
Click	Position the pointer and then quickly press and release the left mouse button.
Double-click	Position the pointer and then quickly press and release the left mouse button twice.
Drag	Position the pointer. Press and hold down the left mouse button as you move the mouse to the desired position. Then release the button.

Mouse pointer shapes

When the mouse is pointed to different parts of the screen, the pointer shape changes, allowing you to perform different tasks. Some commands also change the pointer shape.

The table below lists some common pointer shapes as encountered in Access:

Pointer shape	Meaning
I	The pointer over the text area. Click to position an insertion point where text may be typed.
↖	This pointer appears over menus, non-text areas of windows, inactive windows, scroll bars or toolbar. You can choose a menu and command, or click a button. You can use the pointer to drag to make a selection.

The pointer is over the selection bar, for example, at the edge of a table, or at the left edge of a cell. You can select a cell, a row or several rows.

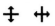 Access is performing a task that will take a few seconds.

 Appears along the borders between window sections or columns. Drag to resize the section or column.

 The pointer appears after you press *Shift-F1*. You can point to any item on the screen and click to view specific Help.

 The pointer is on a window border. Depending on which border, the pointer will assume one of the shapes shown opposite. Drag to resize the window.

 This pointer appears when you have selected the **Move** or **Size** command from the **Control** menu. You can move the window to a new position or drag the window border.

 This pointer appears over the grey bar at the top of a column in a table, query or filter. Click to select the column.

 This pointer appears in the record selection bar. Click to select the record.

 This is the drag and drop pointer which appears when you make a selection and drag the selection to its new location; release the mouse button to drop or insert the selection.

 This is the zoom pointer which appears in print preview.

 The pointer is on a control sizing handle. Depending on which handle, the pointer will assume one of the shapes opposite. Drag to resize the control.

 In form or report design this pointer is used to move an individual label or control.

 In form or report design this pointer is used to move a label and control or a selected set of controls.

 This pointer appears with a Toolbox icon and indicates the position of the control on the form or report design. Click to position the control.

265

Basics of Windows: a quick review

The Windows screen has the following features:

Menu bar

The menu bar shows the titles of the various pull-down menus that are available with a given application. To select a menu option, first select the menu by placing the mouse pointer over the name of the menu on the menu bar and click the left mouse button. The menu will appear. Move the mouse pointer to the menu option you require and click the left mouse button again. Note that any menu options displayed in light grey are not currently available. Menus can also be accessed via the keyboard. For example, to select the file menu press *ALT+F*, i.e. press *ALT* together with the initial letter of the menu option.

Control menu

The **Control** menu is found on all windows, whether they are application windows or document windows. To access the **Control** menu click on the control menu box in the upper left corner of the window, or press *ALT+Spacebar*. The exact contents are different for different windows, but typically basic windows operations such as restore, move, size, minimise, maximise and close are represented.

Title bar

The title bar tells you which window is displayed. By pointing the mouse at the window's title bar, and then dragging the title bar to a new location, the window can be moved.

Task bar

At the bottom of your screen is the task bar. It contains the **Start** button, which you can use to quickly start a program or to find a file. It is also the fastest way to get Help.

When you open a program, document or window, a button appears on the task bar. You can use this button to switch quickly between the windows you have open.

Maximize, minimize and restore buttons

Clicking on the maximize button ⬚ enlarges a window to its maximum size, so that it fills the whole desktop.

Clicking on the restore button ⬚ will restore a maximised window to its previous size.

Clicking on the minimize button ⬚ reduces the window to a small icon at the bottom of the screen. When you shrink an application window to an icon, the application is still running in memory, but its window is not taking up space on your desktop.

Clicking on the Close button ☒ closes the window.

Dialog boxes

Windows uses dialog boxes to request information from you and to provide information to you. Most dialog boxes include options, with each option asking for a different kind of information.

After all of the requested information has been supplied you choose a command button to carry out the command. Two command buttons that feature on every dialog box are **OK** and **Cancel**. **OK** causes the command to be executed; **Cancel** cancels the operation and removes the dialog box from the screen. These buttons represent the two means of quitting from a dialog box. To choose a command button, click on it, or if the button is currently active, press *Enter*.

There are a number of different kinds of controls found in dialog boxes.

■ Text boxes are boxes where you are allowed to type in text, such as a filename. The presence of a flashing vertical bar, or the insertion point, indicates that the text box is active and that you may enter text. If the text box is not active, place the mouse pointer on the box and click. The insertion point will then appear in the box.

■ List boxes show a column of available choices. Items can be selected from a list box by double-clicking on the item, by or clicking once on the item and then clicking on the **OK** button.

■ Check boxes offer a list of options that you can switch on and off. You can select as many or as few check box options as are applicable. When an option in a check box is selected it contains a ✓; otherwise the box is empty. To select a check box, click on the empty box.

Option buttons appear as a list of mutually exclusive items. You can select only one option from the list at a time. You can change a selection by selecting a different button. The selected button contains a black dot. To select an option button, click on it.

Scroll bars appear at the side of windows and list boxes. They appear when the information contained in a window cannot be displayed wholly within that window. Both vertical and horizontal scroll bars may be present depending on whether the database object is too long or too wide to fit on the screen. The small box in the middle of the bar represents the position of the currently displayed screen within the whole object. You can move to a different position in the object by moving this box. You can move this box either by clicking on the scroll bar arrow boxes, clicking on the scroll bar itself or dragging the box.

Data and data definitions

Membership table data:

Membership No	Category	Lastname	Firstname	Title	Street
1	2	Walker	Andrew J	Mr	16 Dovecot Close
2	1	Cartwright	Denise	Mrs	27 Bowling Green Rd
3	6	Perry	Jason R	Mr	59 Church Street
4	2	Forsythe	Ann M	Miss	2 Ferndale Close
5	1	Jameson	Donna	Mrs	25 Alder Drive
6	3	Robinson	Petra	Miss	16 Lowton Lane
7	5	Harris	David J	Mr	55 Coven Road
8	2	Shangali	Imran	Mr	47 High Street
9	1	Barrett	Martha A	Mrs	7 Oldcott Way
10	1	Weiner	George W F	Mr	6 Church Street
11	6	Ali	David	Mr	33 Meirton Road
12	2	Young	Aileen	Ms	78 Highgate Street
13	5	Gray	Ivor P	Mr	4 The Parade
14	5	Swift	Freda	Miss	23 Ferndale Close
15	1	Davies	Sandra M	Mrs	61 Hallfield Road
16	1	Robinson	Rebecca	Mrs	9 Moss Street
17	2	Everett	Alan	Mr	12 Stanley Street
18	4	Locker	Liam	Mr	2 Beech Close
19	4	Locker	Alison	Miss	2 Beech Close
20	1	Jones	Edward R	Mr	17 Mayfield Avenue

	Town	County	Post Code	Telephone No	Occupation	Date of Birth
1	Chelmer	Cheshire	CH2 6TR	01777 569236	Builder	12/3/52
2	Meirton	Cheshire	CH9 2EV	01777 552099	Housewife	29/11/60
3	Chelmer	Cheshire	CH1 8YU			3/6/81
4	Chelmer	Cheshire		01777 569945	Receptionist	5/8/73
5	Chelmer	Cheshire	CH2 7FN		Housewife	4/12/70
6	Branford	Staffs	ST10 2DZ	01778 890523		7/7/84
7	Chelmer	Cheshire	CH3 8PS	01777 569311	Retired	22/5/28
8	Chelmer	Cheshire	CH1 7JH	01777 561553	Accountant	15/3/55
9	Meirton	Cheshire	CH9 3DR	01777 557822	Teacher	25/11/60
10	Chelmer	Cheshire	CH1 8YV		Electrician	10/2/58
11	Chelmer	Cheshire	CH4 5KD	01777 569066		14/7/80
12	Branford	Staffs	ST10 4RT	01778 894471	Civil Servant	25/10/51
13	Chelmer	Cheshire	CH1 7ER	01777 565715	Unemployed	12/4/47
14	Chelmer	Cheshire	CH2 8PN	01777 567351	Retired	14/9/27
15	Meirton	Cheshire	CH9 1YJ	01778 891441	Clerk	1/2/65
16	Chelmer	Cheshire	CH2 8SE	01777 568812	Housewife	18/5/68
17	Chelmer	Cheshire	CH3 3CJ		Draughtsperson	30/7/57
18	Chelmer	Cheshire	CH3 8UH			30/12/83
19	Chelmer	Cheshire	CH3 8UH			30/12/83
20	Chelmer	Cheshire	CH2 9OL	01777 567333	Bus Driver	22/12/58

	Date of Joining	Date of Last Renewal	Sporting Interests	Smoker	Sex
1	3/2/92	3/2/97	Tennis, squash	Yes	Yes
2	16/7/91	16/7/96	Aerobics, swimming, running, squash	No	No
3	12/12/94	12/12/96	Judo, Karate	No	Yes
4	16/9/91	16/9/96		No	No
5	15/6/92	15/6/96	Aerobics, squash	Yes	No
6	3/1/95	3/1/97	Swimming, Judo	No	No
7	1/2/94	1/2/97	Badminton, cricket	Yes	Yes
8	6/4/92	6/4/96	Weight training, squash	No	Yes
9	4/10/93	4/10/96	Keep fit, swimming	No	No
10	15/7/92	15/7/96	Weight training, squash	No	Yes
11	2/10/93	2/10/96	Judo, swimming, football	No	Yes
12	9/8/92	9/8/95	Keep fit, Aerobics, squash	Yes	No
13	5/1/95	5/1/97		Yes	Yes
14	16/9/93	16/9/96		No	No
15	5/4/92	5/4/97	Aerobics, squash, swimming	Yes	No
16	6/12/91	6/12/96	Tennis, Aerobics	No	No
17	5/11/93	5/11/96	Squash, Fitness training, football	No	Yes
18	13/6/92	13/6/97		No	Yes
19	13/6/92	13/6/97		No	No
20	17/5/91	17/5/96	Weight training	Yes	Yes

Membership category table data:

Category No	Category Type	Membership Fee
1	Senior	£25.00
2	Senior Club	£30.00
3	Junior	£10.00
4	Junior Club	£15.00
5	Concessionary	£18.00
6	Youth Club	£20.00

Classes table data:

Class No	Class Day	Class Time	Class Tutor	Class Activity	Male/Female/ Mixed
1	Monday	10:00	Evans	Ladies' Aerobics	Female
2	Monday	11:00	Franks	Weight Training	Male
3	Monday	15:00	Latham	Body Conditioning	Mixed
4	Monday	19:00	Wheildon	Step Aerobics	Mixed
5	Tuesday	10:00	Jackson	Men's Multi-gym	Male
6	Tuesday	14:00	Adams	Ladies' Multi-gym	Female
7	Tuesday	19:00	Jackson	Family Multi-gym	Mixed
8	Wednesday	10:00	Evans	Ladies' Aerobics	Female
9	Wednesday	14:00	Latham	Body Conditioning	Mixed
10	Wednesday	15:00	Franks	Weight training	Female
11	Wednesday	19:00	Franks	Weight Training	Mixed
12	Thursday	11:00	Latham	Weight Training	Male
13	Thursday	14:00	Wheildon	Step Aerobics	Mixed
14	Thursday	15:00	Adams	Multi-gym	Mixed
15	Thursday	19:00	Latham	Body Conditioning	Mixed
16	Friday	10:00	Latham	Body Conditioning	Female
17	Friday	11:00	Wheildon	Step Aerobics	Mixed
18	Friday	14:00	Jackson	Men's Multi-gym	Male

Bookings table data:

Booking No	Room/Hall/Court	Membership No	Class No	Date	Time	Member/ Class
1	Fitness Suite		1	13/5/96	10:00	Class
2	Fitness Suite		2	13/5/96	11:00	Class
3	Sports hall 2		3	13/5/96	15:00	Class
4	Sports hall 1		4	13/5/96	19:00	Class
5	Fitness Suite		5	14/5/96	10:00	Class
6	Fitness Suite		6	14/5/96	14:00	Class
7	Fitness Suite		7	14/5/96	19:00	Class
8	Fitness Suite		8	15/5/96	10:00	Class
9	Sports hall 2		9	15/5/96	14:00	Class
10	Sports hall 2		10	15/5/96	15:00	Class
11	Sports hall 2		11	15/5/96	19:00	Class
12	Sports hall 2		12	16/5/96	11:00	Class
13	Sports hall 2		13	16/5/96	14:00	Class
14	Fitness Suite		14	16/5/96	15:00	Class
15	Sports hall 2		15	16/5/96	19:00	Class
16	Sports hall 2		16	17/5/96	10:00	Class
17	Sports hall 2		17	17/5/96	11:00	Class
18	Fitness Suite		18	17/5/96	14:00	Class
19	Court 1	2		13/5/96	18:00	Member
20	Court 2	17		16/5/96	14:00	Member
21	Court 3	15		14/5/96	11:00	Member
22	Court 1	12		15/5/96	19:00	Member

Class list table data:

Class No	Membership No
1	2
1	5
1	16
4	4
4	6
5	7
5	10
5	1

Data definitions

Bookings table:

Columns

Name	Type	Size
Booking No	AutoNumber	4
Index: Primary key		
Room/Hall/Court	Text	20
Required: True		
Index: Ascending		
Membership No	Number (Long)	4
Class No	Number (Long)	4
Date	Date/Time	8
Required: True		
Format: d/m/yy		
Index: Date+Time		
Time	Date/Time	8
Required: True		
Format: hh:mm Short time		
Index: Date+Time		
Member/Class	Yes/No	1
Required: True		

Classes table:

Columns

Name	Type	Size
Class No	AutoNumber	4
Index: Primary key		
Class Day	Text	10
Required: True		
Class Time	Date/Time	8
Format: hh:mm Short time		

		Text	30
Class Tutor		Text	30
Class Activity		Text	20
	Required: True		
Male/Female/ Mixed		Text	10
	Validation Rule: "Male" or "Female" or "Mixed"		
	Validation Text: Please enter Male, Female or Mixed		

Membership table:

Columns

Name		Type	Size
Membership No		Number (Long)	4
	Description: Automatic membership numbering		
	Index: Primary key		
Category No		Number (Byte)	1
	Description: Categories are 1-Senior, 2-Senior Club, 3-Junior, 4-Junior Club, 5-Concessionary, 6-Youth Club		
	Validation Rule: <=6		
	Validation Text: Please enter a category between 1 and 6		
	Required: True		
Lastname		Text	25
	Required: True		
	Index: Lastname+Firstname		

Firstname		Text	30
	Index: Lastname+Firstname		
Title		Text	10
Street		Text	30
	Required: True		
Town		Text	25
	Default value: Chelmer		
	Required: True		
County		Text	20
	Default value: Cheshire		
	Required: True		
Post Code		Text	10
	Format:>		
Telephone No		Text	12
Occupation		Text	50
Date of Birth		Date/Time	8
	Format: short date		
	Index: Ascending		
Date of Joining		Date/Time	8
	Format: short date		
	Index: Ascending		
Date of Last Renewal		Date/Time	8
	Format: short date		
	Index: Ascending		
Sporting Interests		Memo	0
Smoker		Yes/No	1
	Format: ;"Smoker";"Non-Smoker"		
Sex		Yes/No	1
	Format: ;"Male";"Female"		

Membership Category table:

Columns

Name	Type	Size
Category No	Byte	1
Index: Primary Key		
Category Type	Text	15
Required: True		
Membership Fee	Currency	8
Required: True		

Tutor table:

Columns

Name	Type	Size
Lastname	Text	25
Index: Primary Key		
Initials	Text	3
Title	Text	10
Street	Text	30
Required: True		
Town	Text	25
Default: Chelmer		
Required: True		
County	Text	20
Default: Cheshire		
Required: True		
Post Code	Text	10
Format:>		
Telephone No	Text	12
National Insurance No	Text	10
Date of Birth	Date/Time	8
Format: d/m/yy		
Index: Ascending		
Qualifications	Memo	0

Class List table:

Columns

Name	Type	Size
Class No	Number (Long)	4
Index: Primary Key		
Membership No	Number (Long)	4
Index: Primary Key		

Access toolbar buttons

Database window

Button	Function
New Database	Creates a new database
Open Database	Opens an existing database
Save	Saves database (inactive)
Print	Print definition of highlighted object
Print Preview	Previews the object definition
Spelling	Runs the spell checker
Cut	Removes selection to the clipboard
Copy	Copies selection to the clipboard
Paste	Pastes the contents of clipboard to current position
Format Painter	Copies formatting (inactive)
Undo	Undoes the last action
Office links	Export to MS Word mail merge, document or MS Excel
Analyze	Analyse table, analyse performance, documentor
Large Icons	Lists database objects in large icons for the selected object type
Small Icons	Lists database objects in small icons for the selected object type
List	Lists icons alphabetically
Details	Lists icon details, e.g. size and creation date
Code	Displays a Visual Basic module window
Properties	Displays the general properties of the object that is currently selected
Relationships	Displays the Relationships window
New Object	Create a new table, query, form, report, macro, module. Or launch Auto Form or Auto Report
Help	Displays the Help pointer

Table Design view

Button	Function
Table View	Displays the data in the table in the form of a datasheet
Save	Saves the table
Print	Print (inactive)
Print Preview	Print Preview
Spelling	Spell check (inactive)
Cut	Removes selection to the clipboard
Copy	Copies selection to the clipboard
Paste	Pastes the contents of clipboard to current position
Format Painter	Copies formatting
Undo	Undoes the last action
Primary Key	Sets primary key for selected field(s)
Indexes	Displays the Indexes dialog box
Insert Row	Inserts a row
Delete Row	Deletes a row
Properties	Displays properties of table
Build	Displays a builder for the selected item or property (only enabled if builder available)
Database Window	Displays the Database window
New Object	Creates a new table, query, form, report, macro, module. Or launch Auto Form or Auto Report
Help	Displays the Help pointer

Query Design view

Button	Function
Query View	Displays the data in the query in the form of a datasheet
Save	Saves the query
Print	Print
Print Preview	Print Preview
Spelling	Spell check
Cut	Removes selection to the clipboard
Copy	Copies selection to the clipboard
Paste	Pastes the contents of clipboard to current position
Format Painter	Copies formatting
Undo	Undoes the last action
Query Type	Drop-down list for choice of Select Query (default type of query), Crosstab query for summarising data, Make Table query, Update query, Append query or Delete query
Run	Runs the query
Show Table	Displays the Show Table dialog box for adding tables
Totals	Displays total row in QBE grid for statistical summary
Top Values	Finds the top values in the active query based on a percentage or number of rows
Properties	Displays the properties of the query
Build	Displays the Expression builder
Database Window	Displays the Database window
New Object	Creates a new table, query, form, report, macro, module. Or launches Auto Form or Auto Report
Help	Displays the Help pointer

Datasheet and form view

Button	Function
Table View	Displays table design
Save	Saves the table layout
Print	Prints the datasheet
Print Preview	Displays the print preview
Spelling	Spell check
Cut	Removes selection to clipboard
Copy	Copies selection to clipboard
Paste	Pastes from clipboard to current position
Format Painter	Copies formatting (inactive)
Undo	Undoes the last action
Sort Ascending	Displays records in ascending order of current field
Sort Descending	Displays records in descending order of current field
Filter By Selection	Filters records based on selected data
Filter By Form	Displays a form for the entry of filter criteria
Apply Filter	Displays filtered records
Find	Searches for selected data
New Record	Goto new record
Delete Record	Removes record
Database Window	Displays the Database window
New Object	Creates a new table, query, form, report, macro, module. Or launches Auto Form or Auto Report
Help	Displays the Help pointer

Form design view

Button	Function
Form View	Runs the form
Save	Saves the form
Print Preview	Displays the print preview
Spelling	Spell check
Cut	Removes selection to clipboard
Copy	Copies selection to clipboard
Paste	Pastes from clipboard to current position
Format Painter	Copies formatting from one control to another. Double-click to copy to several controls, *Esc* to finish
Undo	Undoes the last action
Field List	Displays the field list window
Toolbox	Displays the toolbox window
AutoFormat	Applies your choice of predefined formats to the form.
Save As Report	Saves the form as a report
Code	Displays an Access Basic form module in the Module window
Properties	Displays the properties sheet
Build	Displays a builder for the selected item or property (only enabled if builder available)
Database Window	Displays the Database window
New Object	Creates a new table, query, form, report, macro, module. Or launches Auto Form or Auto Report
Help	Displays the Help pointer
Select Object	Selects entire form, section of a form or a control
Font Name	Displays list of font names
Font Size	Displays list of font sizes
Bold	Applies bold typeface
Italic	Applies italic typeface
Underline	Applies underlining

Button	Function
Align Left	Left aligns contents of label or control
Center	Centre aligns contents of label or control
Align Right	Right aligns contents of label or control
Back Color	Drop-down background colour selection
Fore Color	Drop-down foreground colour selection
Border Color	Drop-down border colour selection
Border Width	Drop-down border width selection
Special Effect	Drop-down special effect (raised, sunken etc.) selection

Report design view

Button	Function
Report View	Previews report
Save	Saves the report
Print Preview	Displays a print preview
Spelling	Spell check
Cut	Removes selection to clipboard
Copy	Copies selection to clipboard
Paste	Pastes from clipboard to current position
Format Painter	Copies formatting from one control to another. Double-click to copy to several controls, *Esc* to finish
Undo	Undoes the last action
Field List	Displays the field list window
Toolbox	Displays the toolbox window
Sorting and Grouping	Displays the **Sorting And Grouping** dialog box
AutoFormat	Applies your choice of predefined formats to the report.
Code	Displays an Access Basic report module in the Module window
Properties	Displays the properties sheet
Build	Displays a builder for the selected item or property (only enabled if builder available)

Button	Function
Database Window	Displays the Database window
New Object	Creates a new table, query, form, report, macro, module. Or launches Auto Form or Auto Report
Help	Displays the Help pointer
Select Object	Selects entire report, section of a report or a control
Font Name	Displays list of font names
Font Size	Displays list of font sizes
Bold	Applies bold typeface
Italic	Applies italic typeface
Underline	Applies underlining
Align Left	Left aligns contents of label or control
Center	Centre aligns contents of label or control
Align Right	Right aligns contents of label or control
Back Color	Drop-down background colour selection
Fore Color	Drop-down foreground colour selection
Border Color	Drop-down border colour selection
Border Width	Drop-down border width selection
Special Effect	Drop-down special effect (raised, sunken etc.) selection

Report and form print preview

Button	Function
Print	Prints
Zoom	Toggle to zoom in or out
One Page	Displays print preview, one page format
Two Pages	Displays print preview, two page format
Zoom Control	Controls the amount of magnification
Close Window	Closes preview and returns to design

Button	Function
Merge It	Saves the output of a table, query, form, report or module to a file, and then attaches the file to a message in your electronic mail program
Publish It with MS Word	Saves the output of a table, query, form, report or module to a file in one of the following file formats: Microsoft Excel (.XLS), Rich Text Format (.RTF), or MS-DOS text (.TXT)
Analyse It with MS Excel	Saves the output of a table, query, form, report or module to a file in one of the following file formats: Microsoft Excel (.XLS), Rich Text Format (.RTF), or MS-DOS text (.TXT)
Database Window	Displays the Database window
New Object	Creates a new table, query, form, report, macro module. Or launches Auto Form or Auto Report
Help	Displays the Help pointer

Macro design

Button	Function
Save	Saves the macro
Print	Prints the macro
Print Preview	Displays the print preview
Spelling	Spell check
Cut	Removes selection to clipboard
Copy	Copies selection to the clipboard
Paste	Pastes from clipboard to current position
Format Painter	Copies formatting from one control to another. Double-click to copy to several controls, *Esc* to finish
Undo	Undoes the last action
Macro Names	Displays the Macro Name column in the Macro window
Conditions	Displays the Condition column in the Macro window
Insert Row	Adds a row to the macro sheet
Delete Row	Deletes a row from the macro sheet

Button	Function
Run	Runs the active macro
Single Step	Turns single stepping on or off
Build	Displays a builder for the selected item or property (only enabled if builder available)
Database Window	Displays the Database window
New Object	Creates a new table, query, form, report, macro or module. Or launches Auto Form or Auto Report
Help	Displays the Help pointer

Module design

Button	Function
Insert Module	Inserts a new module into the current database
Insert Procedure	Inserts a procedure declaration statement
Save	Saves the module
Print	Prints the module
Undo	Undoes the last action
Redo	Redoes the last action
Debug Window	Displays a window that can be used to debug code. This window will display values of specified variables
Object Browser	Displays all methods and properties in the current and other available databases
Continue	Continues code execution after it has been suspended
End	Terminates code execution
Reset	Stops execution of procedures and reinitialises code variables
Breakpoint	Sets or removes a breakpoint
Instant Watch	Displays the value of a selected expression
Calls	Displays the Calls dialog box, in which you can trace all the currently active procedures that your code has called
Step Into	Runs one statement at a time, including statements within a called procedure

Button	Function
Step Over	Runs one statement at a time, treating a called procedure as one step
Compile loaded modules	Compiles all procedures in open modules or modules behind open forms and reports
Indent	Shifts selected code or line at the insertion point four spaces to the right, by default
Outdent	Shifts selected code or line at the insertion point four spaces to the left, by default
Build	Displays a builder for the selected item or property (only enabled if builder available)
Database Window	Displays the Database window
New Object	Creates a new table, query, form, report, macro or module. Or launches Auto Form or Auto Report
Help	Displays the Help pointer

Glossary

Action queries	Queries which change the records
Application	A fully operational system
Back colour	Background colour
Bound controls	There are associated with a field on a form that displays or alters data (and see Unbound controls)
Calculated controls	Expressions, usually performing a calculation on data
Calculated field	The result of a series of calculations that a query may be asked to perform
Custom formats	These display particular data (such as dates or telephone numbers) in some particular way, however it is entered
Database application	A set of related database objects used to accomplish a particular task
Delimited text file	Where the fields are separated by some special character, such as a comma or a tab
Dynaset	Records chosen by Access in response to a Select query, q.v.
Events	Actions, such as opening a form, selecting a field control, etc.
Field size	The maximum length of a text field or type of number
Filter	One (alterable) selection stored within each table, used to display particular chosen records
Fore colour	Foreground colour
Grouped report	This puts particular selected fields in a row, and then displays the result as a table; thus taking up less space on a page than a full table
Imported data	Is converted from a non-Access format into Access
Input mask	Data entry pattern designed to help entering lots of similar information
Link data	Data from a non-Access database which behaves as though it is part of the Access table, but remains in its original file format
Main form	A selection from one of the primary tables in the database, see also Subform
Modules	Programs/instructions to perform a particular task or tasks
Null values	Fields in which there is nothing
Parameter queries	These change the criteria for a query
Primary key	A field or fields that uniquely identify each record in an index or table to aid queries

288

Referential integrity	A check that relational data does exist in two (or more) tables
Relationships	These exist when one-to-one, one-to-many, or many-to-many fields match in two or more tables
Screen form	This is used to customise the displaying of records and queries on the screen
Select queries	Questions the user wishes to ask about entries in fields
Snap-to-grid	When on, this automatically aligns new controls on a form to points on the grid
Style enhancements	Presentational improvements for text, such as alignment, colour, three-dimensionality, fonts, borders, etc.
Subform	One deriving its data from a Main form, q.v.
Template	This determines the default settings for form, report, section and control properties, etc.
Unbound controls	These are associated with parts of a form (such as labels) which are independent of data. Cf. Bound controls
Validation rules	Tests on entries designed to ensure the accuracy of data as it is entered
Zero length	A string of characters indicating that data exists but is unknown

Index